A WOMAN'S GUIDE TO SPIRIT-FILLED LIVING

A Woman's Guide to Spirit-Filled Living

❦

Quin Sherrer and Ruthanne Garlock

VINE BOOKS

Servant Publications
Ann Arbor, Michigan

Vine Books is an imprint of Servant Publications especially designed to serve evangelical Christians.

Unless otherwise noted, all Scripture quotations in this book are from *The Holy Bible: New International Version*, © 1973, 1978, 1984, International Bible Society. Used by permission of Zondervan Bible Publishers. Other versions quoted are abbreviated as follows: *TAB, The Amplified Bible*, Zondervan Publishing; *NKJ, New King James Version*, Thomas Nelson Publishers; *PHI, The New Testament in Modern English*, by J. B. Phillips, Geoffrey Bles, Ltd.; *TLB, The Living Bible Paraphrased*, Tyndale House Publishers; *NAS, New American Standard*.

The circumstances of certain events and some names of persons and locations have been changed to protect individuals' privacy.

Published by Servant Publications, P.O. Box 8617, Ann Arbor, Michigan 48107

Cover design: Left Coast Design, Inc., Portland, Oregon
Cover illustration: Krieg Barrie

Printed in the United States of America
ISBN 0-89283-934-1

"Once again, two of the most respected women of God in this hour have written another practical, yet profound, book for women. This guide is born of their experience and has insights and personal anecdotes to bring encouragement, understanding, authenticity, and clarity to every woman desiring to live the Spirit-filled life."

ELIZABETH (BETH) ALVES
PRESIDENT, INTERCESSORS INTERNATIONAL

"*A Woman's Guide to Spirit-Filled Living* is a must for busy women. Quin and Ruthanne have linked the beauty of a woman and the power of God at work with her. There are many life-giving illustrations that are invaluable to the reader. I enjoyed it immensely."

BOBBYE BYERLE
U.S. NATIONAL PRESIDENT, AGLOW INTERNATIONAL

"This is an extremely informative book and is well-balanced in its practical approach to the Spirit-filled life. It is easily readable and will surely be a helpful tool for the new believer as well as the mature believer. Many will find it a MUST for their libraries."

PASTOR TED HAGGARD
NEW LIFE CHURCH, COLORADO SPRINGS, CO

"Inspiration, encouragement, and everyday help for and from women who value walking in the Spirit."

RUSSELL P. SPITTLER
PROVOST AND PROFESSOR OF NEW TESTAMENT
FULLER THEOLOGICAL SEMINARY, PASADENA, CA

"*A Woman's Guide to Spirit-Filled Living* is a wonderful gift to the body of Christ! It unfolds deep truth and empower women of all kinds for fruitful ministry by a lavish use of inspiring anecdotes of anointed women who are serving God in remarkable ways. Whether you are a man or woman, my friends, Quin and Ruthanne will touch your heart and move you to action in an unforgettable way."

C. PETER WAGNER
FULLER THEOLOGICAL SEMINARY, PASADENA, CA

In memory of Quin's mother
Jewett Lammon Moore
and
In honor of Ruthanne's mother
Hazel McBee Sandidge

Along with a company of other women mentors and teachers who have faithfully encouraged us and taught us valuable lessons about Spirit-filled living.

I (Quin) especially thank the Reverend Forrest Mobley and the Reverend Peter Lord for enriching my prayer walk over many years, and my current pastor, Reverend Dutch Sheets, for his encouragement and prayer coverage.

I (Ruthanne) express appreciation for the godly nurture and mentoring I received from the late Reverends John and Lydia Stubblefield, who introduced me to the Holy Spirit and were my pastors during my growing-up years.

Other Books by the Authors

How to Forgive Your Children
How to Pray for Your Family and Friends
A Woman's Guide to Spiritual Warfare
The Spiritual Warrior's Prayer Guide
A Woman's Guide to Breaking Bondages
by
Quin Sherrer and Ruthanne Garlock

A Christian Woman's Guide to Hospitality
(formerly *A House of Many Blessings*)
by
Quin Sherrer and Laura Watson

How to Pray for Your Children
by
Quin Sherrer

Before We Kill and Eat You
Fire in His Bones
by
Ruthanne Garlock

The Christian in Complete Armour, volumes 1-3
Ruthanne Garlock was the senior editor for the abridged edition
of this Puritan classic written by William Gurnall in 1655.

Contents

A WOMAN'S GUIDE TO SPIRIT-FILLED LIVING

Introduction

✤

This book's very existence is a tangible result of the work of the Holy Spirit. He has proved to us personally (Quin and Ruthanne) that he can bring renewal to individual believers, impart his gifts to members of the body of Christ, and bring unity among Christians from widely diverse theological backgrounds.

We've learned that Spirit-filled living means much more than embracing a textbook theology of the Holy Spirit.

I (Ruthanne) grew up in the Pentecostal tradition and graduated from a Pentecostal Bible college. Everything in my background tended to make me feel that my denomination had a superior understanding of spiritual truth.

Almost all my relatives in both my parents' families were members of the denomination that Mom and Dad had left when they were baptized in the Holy Spirit. I always felt they looked down on us because of our beliefs. The same went for my peers in public school, where I had very few close friends. But of course I thought—since they refused to accept what I believed about the Holy Spirit—that *they* were inferior. How perverse spiritual pride can be!

I (Quin), on the other hand, came from the opposite end of the denominational spectrum. Going back for generations, my ancestors had been ministers in a mainline, traditional church. I believed that Pentecostals not only were wrong in their doctrine, but also bordered on being "crazy" because of their practice of speaking in tongues.

Normally, we *never* could have ended up being friends, much less prayer partners and co-writers. But we've come to see that admitting mistakes, laying aside pride and dogmatic ideas, and opening up to the inner work of the Holy Spirit and his revelation of the Word of God, overcomes formidable barriers. Both of us have changed in the way we look at ourselves, the way we view other believers, and the way we understand the Holy Spirit.

We've learned that in our desire for spiritual gifts, we must follow the way of love (see 1 Corinthians 14:1). In doing this, we can fulfill Jesus' command that we love one another so the world will know we are his followers (see John 13:34-35).

You will meet in the pages of this book scores of women whose lives have been touched and transformed by the power of the Holy Spirit. You will meet women of the Bible, women from recent history, and women like those in your neighborhood. You will discover that women believers—no matter our race, our culture, our time-slot in history, or our religious background—have a common bond in the person of Jesus Christ and the work of his Holy Spirit.

In essence, Spirit-filled living means endeavoring to live as Jesus lived when he walked on the earth.

—Quin Sherrer and Ruthanne Garlock
Dallas, Texas, January 1996

ONE

Welcoming the Holy Spirit

*When [Peter and John] arrived, they prayed for [the
Samaritans] that they might receive the Holy Spirit, because
the Holy Spirit had not yet come upon any of them; they had
simply been baptized into the name of the Lord Jesus.*

Acts 8:15-16

By inviting the Holy Spirit to work more deeply in our lives,
we who long for more of God can discover a new level of
supernatural living. That's what I (Quin) experienced one
night in a little church in Destin, Florida. I'd gone to Destin to
visit my mother and there I learned that the Holy Spirit desires
to completely dwell in every believer.

Revealing New Truth

The worship service was foreign to me. Men and women
were raising their hands in praise to God. The congregation
began to sing from the Bible. To me, it was mind-boggling. I
frowned and gave Mom a questioning look during the singing.
"Those are scripture choruses," she whispered, smiling and
joining in.

I'd reluctantly agreed to visit St. Andrews Episcopal Church
with Mom simply because she insisted it was a good way to
spend a Thursday night. Besides, she wanted me to meet some
of her new friends during my visit.

She had reared us in a liturgical church—though it wasn't

Episcopal. I don't remember a time when I didn't love Jesus or pray to the Father. But the Holy Spirit was barely mentioned.

I was accustomed to a fixed form of worship, beginning with the congregation singing the Doxology:

> *Praise God, from whom all blessings flow;*
> *Praise Him, all creatures here below;*
> *Praise Him above, ye heavenly host:*
> *Praise Father, Son, and Holy Ghost.*

The minister always opened with prayer, followed by our singing three lovely old hymns, reverently placing our offering in silver plates, listening to a twenty-minute sermon, and leaving after the benediction. One hour on Sunday morning and we were ready for lunch.

I was now in my thirties with three children, and my husband and I were rearing them in the same tradition. But here, in this crowded little church with people standing in the aisles, I was introduced to the *presence* of the Holy Spirit for the first time.

I watched in amazement as a grown man, with hands upraised, began softly praising the Lord as tears rolled down his cheeks. "Jesus, I love you. Jesus, I praise you. Jesus, I thank you for providing a way to heaven for me," he whispered. The sights and sounds captivated me. Though the service lasted more than two hours, it seemed like only moments. In my heart I knew these people knew Jesus at a depth that I didn't. And I yearned to have what they had.

Upon leaving the meeting I swallowed my stiff-necked pride. "What makes these people so different from me and other Christians I know?" I asked the pastor, Forrest Mobley. "I've taught Sunday School most of my life, and Jesus is my Savior. But I don't worship like these folks. How can I do it?"

"Most of these who come to worship on Thursday night have received the baptism in the Holy Spirit—the gift Jesus told his followers he would send before he went back to heaven," Pastor Mobley told me.

"You mean I can receive it, too?" I asked.

"Of course you can," he responded. "After our Thursday meetings, those who are interested in more instruction can come to my office. First I teach, then pray for them to be filled with power—or as Jesus called it, 'baptized with the Holy Spirit.'"

"I'll have to give this more thought," I said, shaking his hand. I was wondering silently, *Is this Holy Spirit the same as the Holy Ghost we sing about in the Doxology?*

"Well, if you're serious," the pastor interrupted my thoughts, "re-read the first four chapters of Acts, then come ask me more questions. But read with an open mind, asking God to reveal the truth to you," he admonished. Since I'd be visiting Mom another ten days, I promised to do that.

Healing Prayer

The next night I attended a home prayer meeting where a group from St. Andrews had gathered. As about a dozen of us sat or knelt in prayer, the telephone rang. Betty, our hostess, slipped out to answer the phone in the hall while everyone else kept on praying. Everyone, that is, except me. Being unaccustomed to praying aloud, I just sat there listening.

Some were praying softly in languages I'd never heard before. Others were thanking God for healing some man named Bill. These people talked to God as if they knew Him intimately! I envied them, yet it bewildered me. Betty re-entered the room and announced softly, "That was a message about Bill Lance. The doctors at the Air Force hospital in Mississippi say he is dying tonight. Let's pray in agreement right now for his life to be spared."

Then Betty prayed aloud while the others listened. "Lord, we've already had a healing service for Bill at our church. Now we believe you are restoring him, regardless of what the doctors say. So we stand in agreement and thank you in advance for his healing."

Someone in the room spoke aloud. "Satan, we give notice that you and your demonic forces cannot have Bill Lance. He is God's property and we are standing in the gap for his complete healing. Spirits of infirmity, leave him, in Jesus' name."

Betty leaned toward me and quietly explained that Bill Lance was a new Christian, a thirty-one-year-old Air Force captain stationed at a nearby base. "He and his wife Sharon have two young children," she said. "The doctors say he's dying with acute leukemia. Tonight he's in critical condition, so prayer groups all over town are being called. But we've had the assurance God is going to heal Bill. He's got the assurance, too, so we'll keep on praying."

I bowed my head and prayed in my heart, *Lord, listen to Betty's prayers—to all their prayers—just count mine out. I don't know whether you still heal today, but I'm willing to learn, Lord. Show me.*

I was really puzzled. Was God still in the healing business? I'd been taught in my church that healing went out with the apostles, along with that part in the New Testament about speaking in tongues. Yet tonight, I sensed something dynamic in the way these people prayed.

Those in the room went on to pray for others with a boldness I'd never encountered. Before the meeting ended, I was sure I wanted to know Jesus as personally as they did. And I wanted to pray and praise God in my own prayer language.

Is Jesus Really My Lord?

I knew Jesus was my Savior, but now I questioned whether I'd allowed him to be Lord. Definitely not, I decided. Whether this was theologically correct or not, this was the way I looked at my life. The following Thursday night I was back at St. Andrews, and after the meeting joined a handful of others in the pastor's study for more instruction.

"Turn to the first chapter of Acts," Pastor Mobley instructed us. Then he read the verses which in my Bible were printed in red ink—indicating Jesus' own words to his disciples:

Do not leave Jerusalem, but wait for the gift my Father promised, which you have heard me speak about. For John baptized with water, but in a few days you will be baptized with the Holy Spirit... you will receive power when the Holy Spirit comes on you; and you will be my witnesses in Jerusalem, and in all Judea and Samaria, and to the ends of the earth. (Acts 1:4b,5,8)

"The Holy Spirit was a gift Jesus promised to his disciples," Pastor Mobley commented. "Today, we also are his disciples. Now let's read what happened after his ascension when the followers of Jesus—120 strong—waited in the Upper Room for this power the Lord promised."

After reading several verses from Acts 2, he began to enumerate the events recorded:

1. Those who gathered were in one accord.

2. They heard a sound like a violent wind come from heaven.

3. They saw what seemed to be tongues of fire resting on each person present.

4. All of them were filled with the Holy Spirit.

5. They began to speak in other tongues as the Spirit enabled them.

"Although his eleven closest disciples had been with Jesus almost constantly for some three years, he still told them and the other followers to 'stay in the city until you have been clothed with power from on high,'" (Lk 24:49) the pastor said. Why? Because they were going to need the power of the Holy Spirit once Jesus ascendedto heaven.

"Tonight we are going to pray together, confess our sins, and ask the Holy Spirit to be in charge of our lives. Then you will receive a new prayer language. Praying in tongues bypasses our minds, enabling our spirits to speak directly to God through the Holy Spirit."

A Night Never to Forget

What followed the Bible lesson that night in Pastor Mobley's office almost 25 years ago totally changed my life. He asked us to put into our own words a prayer something like this one:

I acknowledge you, Jesus, as my Lord and Savior. I ask you to forgive my sins: the wrong things I've done, and things I've failed to do; the things I remember and those I don't. I choose to forgive all who have hurt or wounded me; I free them from any bondage I've held them in through my unforgiveness. If I have ever made fun of anyone who spoke in tongues, please forgive me. Lord, I receive your forgiveness for my sins.

Now I renounce any involvement with the occult (horoscopes, mind-reading, fortune-telling, etc.) and ask for your forgiveness. I renounce the devil and all his works.

Lord, I now ask to receive the baptism in the Holy Spirit and to speak in a new tongue. In the name of Jesus Christ, I receive in faith. Amen.

Pastor Mobley then laid hands on each of us and prayed that the spiritual gifts from 1 Corinthians 12:8-10 would be imparted to us as he called them out: word of wisdom, word of knowledge, faith, healing, working of miracles, prophecy, discerning of spirits, various kinds of tongues, interpretation of tongues. Then he asked God to give us the fruit of the Spirit as mentioned in Galatians 5.

I timidly spoke only three little unfamiliar syllables. They sounded so elementary to me. Was this really praying in tongues, or did I make it up? How glad I was for the warning Pastor Mobley gave after the meeting.

"Don't let the devil tell you you did not speak in tongues tonight," he cautioned. "God gave you that gift of the Holy Spirit. And just as a baby learns to talk with only a few sounds at first, so your prayer language begins with a few syllables, then will expand, increase, and often change."

It was a night I was never to forget. Bells didn't go off, nor did sweat break out in my palms. But an overpowering love for God and people began to engulf me—especially love and forgiveness for my dad, who had abandoned our family when I was twelve years old.

Renewal Hits Home

When I left Mom's place to return home a few days later, I was definitely changed. I laughed more. I studied the Bible with a new hunger. I even started praying for some close friends to be healed. And amazingly, some were healed instantly!

The Holy Spirit was so real to me, the words of familiar church hymns now held new meaning. I sang the *Gloria Patri*—dating from the second-century church—with joy and enthusiasm:

> *Glory be to the Father,*
> *And to the Son, and to the Holy Ghost.*
> *As it was in the beginning,*
> *Is now, and ever shall be,*
> *World without end, Amen. Amen!*

I also had a new appreciation for the first question from the Westminster Catechism: "Q: What is the chief end of man?" "A: Man's chief end is to glorify God and enjoy him forever." I'd memorized this as a child, but now I was learning what it means to glorify God, and I was enjoying his presence in my life.

My husband, LeRoy, who was an elder in our church, watched me for six months. Finally one day he walked up behind me and put his arms around me while I was in the kitchen. "Whatever happened to you when you visited your Mom last summer, I need it too," he said. "You've changed so much, and I want to have the same experience."

"It's called the baptism of the Holy Spirit," I smiled. "But I honestly don't know how to help you receive it—I'm too new myself. Let's call a pastor I have heard about in Orlando and ask him to pray with you."

After special prayer, LeRoy received the baptism of the Holy Spirit and spoke in tongues. Then he began loving and encouraging others as he'd never done before. Now, when I wanted to go hear a Christian speaker—even a hundred miles away—he would drive me. But we didn't go alone. We loaded up our station wagon with our children and friends who expressed a spiritual hunger. Before long we were hosting two Bible studies a week in our home.

Miracle Story

The following summer, when I returned to Destin to visit Mom, I stopped at the church office the first afternoon to see Pastor Mobley.

"Quin, come back here and meet Bill Lance; I think you should write his testimony since he's our church's first healing miracle," he exclaimed when he saw me. (I'd been writing people's stories for a number of years.) "Remember how we were all praying for Bill to be healed from leukemia last summer?"

I followed him into the church library, expecting to meet an emaciated man with thinning hair. Instead, the man dressed in jeans and a sport shirt who thrust his hand out to shake mine was robust and exuberant. His round face glowed with health and happiness, and he had a thick mane of hair.

As all three of us settled on the couch, Bill told me his miracle story. A short time later, I wrote his healing testimony and the story won the prestigious *Guideposts* Magazine Writer's Contest, enabling me to learn from the best of Christian writers at *Guideposts* in New York. From there my career changed from writing for a local newspaper to writing for Christian magazines, and eventually to writing books. I would laugh and tell people, "My new boss is a Jewish carpenter!"

I'm happy to report that all these years later, Bill Lance is still very much alive and well. He has established his own business and now lives in Colorado, not far from us. And Pastor Mobley is still praying for folks to receive the baptism of the Holy Spirit.

I am no longer hesitant to introduce people to Jesus or to pray for their healing. My prayer language has definitely become fluent since those first halting syllables. In fact, I've prayed for scores of people to receive this gift.

Misunderstood or Persecuted

But I must caution you to expect misunderstanding when you begin to stand for Spirit-filled living. The Apostle Paul wrote, "Persecution is inevitable for those who are determined to live really Christian lives" (2 Tm 3:12 PHI).

Some persecution will no doubt come from family members or church friends who don't understand your new fervor for God. You may well be ridiculed or even accused of being a religious fanatic.

That was my experience back in the early '70s after I received the Holy Spirit. Some church friends just didn't understand what had happened to me. At one dinner party an elder from my church criticized me, saying tongues were relevant only for the New Testament church, not today. "How can you even believe that the devil is still active today?" he asked in disbelief. Another questioned why I now took my Bible to church, implying that I was checking to see if the preacher was quoting it accurately. Even the pastor called me into his office and cautioned me not to raise my hands in worship because it would bother the choir. He had heard about the way charismatics worship.

Looking back, I know I was not always wise about when and how I shared about my encounter with the Holy Spirit. I was so excited, I wanted all my close friends to know that this gift was available for them too.

After one particular barrage of persecution, I phoned Pastor Mobley back in Destin for counsel and prayer. "Quin," he said, "God didn't promise us a rose garden, and even if he did, there are plenty of thorns in one. Why don't you read some New Testament scriptures on persecution and tribulations? And be careful not to hold any grudges. I'll be praying for you."

His counsel wasn't particularly comforting, but I tried to follow it.

Two years later when Pastor Mobley came to Titusville to visit LeRoy and me and to pray with us, we all three felt God was releasing us to a new phase in our walk with the Lord. We could now move to another church. Pastor Peter Lord of Park Avenue Baptist Church agreed to give us oversight and we joined his church. From his teaching came inspiration for some of my books. While his was not known as a charismatic church, he accepted LeRoy and me just as we were. He even approved of our teaching about the operation of the gifts of the Spirit in our home Bible studies. I will be forever grateful to him.

Power to Witness

Jesus declared that after receiving the Holy Spirit, his followers would have power to be his witnesses (see Acts 1:8).

I found that now I had the boldness to share the Lord and pray with people—something I had never done before. I talked to school teachers, the principal, my mailman, my butcher, people in the supermarket. I even asked my newspaper editor, for whom I'd worked many years, to allow me to write a "Fortress of Faith" page each Friday to include Christian testimonies of community leaders and feature articles on local pastors and their churches. This gave me the opportunity to meet almost every pastor in town, and all I wanted to talk about was Jesus— and my newfound love for him.

My best friend, Lib, who with her husband had gone with us to several full gospel meetings, watched me with great curiosity for several months. Finally she admitted she too yearned for the baptism of the Holy Spirit. "But I'm just not good enough, Quin—I can't ask Jesus for this gift," she kept telling me. I couldn't convince her the gift was for her.

One day she said it again, crying buckets of tears. I looked her in the eyes and said, "No, Lib, you aren't good enough. I'm not. No one is. But if the Father says he will give good gifts to his children, you are one of his children, entitled to a good gift. The Holy Spirit wants to be your helper, teacher, and encourager. And he wants to pray through you. Now, just ask him sometime when you're alone."

"OK—I'll do it," she said. A short time later Lib and her husband, Gene, were in church on Wednesday night listening to their pastor's message. Suddenly the Holy Spirit sovereignly moved upon both of them at the same time, and they began weeping. As they yielded to the Holy Spirit they both received their prayer language.

After that Lib and I began to pray together on the phone every weekday morning at 8:00 for five minutes. Our focus: to pray for our children. How glad I was that both my husband and my best friend were now enjoying the fullness of the Spirit.

Lib and I were prayer partners for years to come.

Rest and Release

Soon after receiving the baptism of the Holy Spirit I got a copy of John Sherrill's book, *They Speak With Other Tongues*, and devoured it. Few books were available in those days to explain how the Holy Spirit was changing the lives of contemporary Christians. Because he was a member of a mainline denomination, I respected what he said. And I gave away copies by the dozens.

In Sherrill's book I read testimonies of those whom he had interviewed and asked, "What is the *use* of speaking in tongues?" A housewife's response: "What's the use of a bluebird? What is the use of a sunset? Just sheer unmitigated uplift, just joy unspeakable and with it health and peace and rest and release from burdens and tension."[1]

A minister told him how he was able to rest while traveling: "... the minute I close my eyes I begin to pray in the Spirit. I pray all night that way, waking up and drifting back to sleep, always praying. I don't get much sleep, but I get a lot of rest. The next morning I'm fresh and strong and ready for a full day's work."[2]

After that, whenever I'd wake at night I would pray in tongues, just like that minister, and found I also awoke very refreshed. I knew two things were happening when I prayed this way: first, I was building myself up in the Holy Spirit (see Jude 1:20); and second, some of the time I was interceding in the Spirit for others (see Romans 8:27).

Sherrill's book also encouraged me because he'd approached the subject as a reporter and ended up receiving the baptism of the Holy Spirit himself. From his many interviews with those who had this experience he made a conclusion:

> Of all the variety of experience with the Holy Spirit, one thing held true in every case. Whether the baptism came quietly or with a bang, unexpectedly or after long seeking, the ultimate result was to draw the individual closer to Christ. Jesus was no longer a figure on the pages of a history book. Nor, even a memory from some personal mountaintop experience. His Spirit was with the baptized believer in a present-time, minute-by-minute way, showing him at every turn the nature and personality of Christ.[3]

Teaching fifth grade girls and boys in Sunday School became an exhilarating time for me to impart something new and fresh to them. Not only did the pages of the Bible spring to life, but so did church history.

Within four months after receiving the baptism, I went to Israel to walk where Jesus and Peter and Paul had walked. And within the year when I won the *Guideposts* writer's contest, I found myself sitting at a table with teachers John and Elizabeth Sherrill, learning some of their writing secrets. As John talked, I was inspired that from now on, when I wrote, I'd pray in the Spirit as I worked. I've tried to continue that practice, as I want to allow the Spirit to flow through me with his creativity.

The Breath of God

Bible teacher Gerald Rowlands reminds us that the word for *spirit* is the same as the Greek word for *breath*. The Hebrew equivalent is *wind*. Pastor Rowlands gives this instruction for those who want to be baptized in the Holy Spirit:

Just as you open your mouth to drink water, you can also open your mouth to drink in the Spirit. Open your mouth and breathe in, and as you do, believe that the Holy Spirit is coming into your life in a new way. Do it in faith.

... There may or may not be an emotional accompaniment. If there is, relax and enjoy it. If there is not, then do not worry about it. Emotions are very erratic and unreliable. The important thing is not what you feel. It is what you believe. *Believe* that you have received the Spirit.

... Speaking in tongues is a miracle. It is a supernatural ability given by the Spirit. This does not mean that it is difficult to do. It simply means that you must cooperate with God.

... We use our tongue and lips in just the same way we do when we speak our native language. The miracle is not in the physical act of speaking. The miracle is in the *language* that we are given to speak. In other words, it is not *how* you speak, but *what* you speak, that is a miracle.... When you speak in tongues, the physical part of it is just as natural as any other time you exercise your powers of speech.[4]

Invite Him to Fill You, Too

Our prayer is that soon you can say with Ruthanne and me that the Holy Spirit is as real to you as your best friend. May you too experience sweet fellowship with him on a regular basis.

The Holy Spirit desires to completely dwell in every believer. But he is gentle, not pushy. The Holy Spirit responds to invitations. If you hunger for more of God, we urge you to pray the prayer that Quin prayed that night in the pastor's study, and open your heart to receive all he desires to give you.

The basic steps to follow are:

1. Confess and repent of any sin in your life. Forgive anyone who has ever hurt you, disappointed you, or falsely accused you. Ask the Lord to remind you of any resentment you may be harboring, and release it through prayer (read Mark 11:22-26 and Ephesians 4:25-32).

2. Ask the Lord to reveal to you any involvement you may have had with the occult (read Deuteronomy 7:25-26; 18:10-12; Acts 19:19-20). Repent and ask forgiveness, no matter how naive you may have been when you participated in an occult activity. Receive God's forgiveness, then renounce the devil and all his works in your life.

3. If you have ever mocked or made fun of anyone who spoke in tongues—even in casual joking—ask God to forgive you for not honoring the Holy Spirit.

4. Ask for the infilling of the Holy Spirit with the ability to pray in tongues. Then open your mouth and begin to speak the syllables the Holy Spirit gives you to say. One of the best ways to receive is through singing. Many receive their prayer language by beginning to sing the simple chorus, "Hallelujah, Hallelujah, Hallelujah... " and then singing syllables to that tune as the Holy Spirit enables them.

5. Use your prayer language every day. It helps you to keep in touch with the Lord, and it builds up your spirit. As you exercise this gift you will become less and less self-conscious and more fluent in your prayer language.

God's Incredible Gift

He [Jesus] told them... "*I am going to send you what my Father has promised; but stay in the city until you have been clothed with power from on high.*"

Luke 24:46,49

- Do you long to have a passionate, intimate, dynamic relationship with God?
- Do you want to know without doubt God's comfort, unconditional love, protection, guidance, renewal, and empowering?
- Do you feel unable to draw upon God's help in times of difficulty?

If your answer is "Yes!" then you are a woman who wants to experience Spirit-filled living. You are a candidate not only to receive the gift of the Holy Spirit, but also to live with the Spirit's power as a daily reality.

The Enemy Robs Our Blessings

In our previous books we have stated that Satan, God's enemy and ours, maligns God's character and tries to cause us to fear rather than trust him. Satan also provokes misunderstanding and disagreement regarding the person and power of the Holy Spirit, thus robbing from vast numbers of Christians the blessings of God's gift.

Many women tell us they are confused by conflicting ideas

about the role of the Holy Spirit in a believer's life, so they're not sure how to distinguish between the works of the Holy Spirit and the works of an alien spirit. Yet they have a craving thirst for more of God's presence and power in their lives.

The Lord himself provides the answer for those who have such yearning:

> ... Jesus stood and said in a loud voice, "If a man is thirsty, let him come to me and drink. Whoever believes in me, as the Scripture has said, streams of living water will flow from within him." By this he meant the Spirit, whom those who believed in him were later to receive. Up to that time the Spirit had not been given, because Jesus had not yet been glorified. (John 7:37-39)

Thirsty for More

Perhaps you can identify with our friend Katy, who had been a Christian since her early teens. Newly graduated from college, she had just received her officer's commission in the Army as a nurse. That summer, while chatting with the woman ahead of her in the food line at a church picnic, the woman said, "The Lord has been speaking to me a lot lately about the Holy Spirit."

"What is the Holy Spirit?" Katy asked, instantly feeling a spark of curiosity.

The woman went on to tell how she had been baptized in the Holy Spirit, had spoken in tongues, and was learning about the gifts and the power of the Holy Spirit.

"I knew the 'Holy Ghost' was included in the Apostles' Creed which I recited every Sunday, and was mentioned at baptisms and in benediction prayers," Katy reported. "But I'd never heard a Bible lesson or sermon about the Holy Spirit. My relationship with Christ was genuine, but I was thirsty for more—especially at this hinge-point in my life."

For five weeks Katy sought in every way possible to learn

more about the Holy Spirit. One night at a meeting of the Officers' Christian Fellowship she was full of questions.

"Would you like to receive the Holy Spirit?" the Bible teacher asked after answering several queries.

"Yes!" Katy responded eagerly, following the Bible teacher and her husband to a back room for prayer.

They laid hands on her and prayed, and led Katy in a prayer asking the Holy Spirit to fill her to overflowing. She did not speak in tongues, but suddenly felt an overwhelming sense of God's love and peace. The experience so changed Katy's demeanor that her colleagues noticed the difference the next day.

A Stream of Strength

"I was so thrilled with this marvelous peace, I decided it wasn't really necessary for me to speak in tongues," she said. "But the couple who had prayed for me to receive the Holy Spirit encouraged me to remain open to tongues without applying a lot of pressure. I learned a lot about the gifts of the Holy Spirit and the many ways he works in our lives. They *showed me* both the fruit and the power of the Holy Spirit."

Six months later, at an officers' Christmas party, another friend prayed for Katy to receive her prayer language, and she haltingly spoke a few words. "A fluency in tongues didn't come right away because of my resistance," she admitted. "But later, when I began struggling with problems in my marriage, I began to pray in tongues when I was alone. Gradually it began to flow more easily. Rather than a 'gusher' experience such as some of my friends had experienced, it seemed the Holy Spirit was 'drip-feeding' me with a steady stream of strength and courage on a day-to-day basis."

Katy discovered that receiving this gift was not just an event—though her first encounter with the Holy Spirit was a spiritual milestone she will always remember. Rather, she's learned that the Holy Spirit living within her enables her to tap into his strength, wisdom, and power as she encounters life's challenges. Today, many years later, Katy prays in tongues in all kinds of situations, but she still prefers to use this gift when she is praying alone, rather than in a group.

Reborn by the Spirit

If you are truly born again, it was the Holy Spirit who convicted you of sin, revealed to you the truth of the gospel, and drew you into relationship with Christ. The following verses emphasize this truth:

> For you did not receive a spirit that makes you a slave again to fear, but you received the Spirit of sonship. And by him we cry, *"Abba,* Father." The Spirit himself testifies with our spirit that we are God's children. (Romans 8:15-16)
> ... No one who is speaking by the Spirit of God says, "Jesus be cursed," and no one can say, "Jesus is Lord," except by the Holy Spirit. (1 Corinthians 12:3)

The Holy Spirit is definitely in you from the time of your conversion. But the baptism of the Holy Spirit we're speaking about, and which Katy received, is subsequent to the salvation experience, as Pastor Jack Hayford explains:

> The Holy Spirit's power must be "received"; it is not an automatic experience. As surely as the Holy Spirit indwells each believer (Romans 8:9), so surely will He fill and overflow each who receives the Holy Spirit in childlike faith (John 7:37-39). When the Holy Spirit fills you, you will know it. Jesus said it and the disciples found it true (Acts 1:4; 2:1-4).[1]

How Do We Respond to This Gift?

The Holy Spirit can be described in many ways, but he is repeatedly referred to as a *gift.* And anyone who accepts Jesus

Christ as Savior and asks him for the gift of the Holy Spirit is eligible to receive it.

The ways we respond upon receiving this gift are as varied as the Holy Spirit's ways of working in our lives. Katy found that the Holy Spirit sustained her with his strength. Several other friends shared with us their feelings and responses when they received the Holy Spirit:

- "I was so wrapped in the love of Jesus, I wanted to stay enfolded in his arms forever," Dorothy told us. "It was like the day I got married, had my first baby placed in my arms, and enjoyed the best Christmas ever—all rolled into one. I wanted to rush up and down my street telling everyone about Jesus, the Lord of my life."

- Ceci received the Holy Spirit at age fourteen and it completely changed her life. "I had an intense hunger for the Bible—I couldn't get enough," she said. "I led many classmates to the Lord and matured beyond my years in Bible knowledge. My Mom wasn't sure what to make of this, so she just watched me. But she liked the fruit she saw in my life because I never went into teenage rebellion."

- Lynn's response was musical. "Now when I play the piano I play melodies as the Holy Spirit gives them to me, and sing praises to God in my prayer language," she reported. "This new experience came after I received the baptism in the Holy Spirit."

- Kay, who had suffered abuse as a child, really never knew what it was like to be loved. She had accepted Christ as her Savior, but was struggling to overcome drug and alcohol addictions, unforgiveness, anger, and rage that tormented her. She'd decided that living the Christian life was just too difficult and had given up. At one point in her struggle a minister had laid hands on her and prayed for her to receive the Holy Spirit. Four years after that prayer, his divine presence literally "invaded" her car and she began speaking in tongues as she was driving.

Pulling to the side of the road, Kay prayed in tongues for more than two hours, and felt the Holy Spirit set her free from every bondage that had hindered her walk with the Lord. After returning home she continued for three days to speak in tongues almost continually.

"Then I understood that I could give up striving to overcome in my own strength," she reported. "Now, as I yield to the Holy Spirit and allow him to work in my heart, I can relax and enjoy his friendship and his presence. Experiencing that sense of the Holy Spirit's closeness and friendship in my life causes me to know I'm loved and accepted by the Father just as I am."

- After being challenged to read the book of Acts, Diane realized she lacked power. "I see now that the Holy Spirit *is* power," she said. "Praying in tongues has given me boldness to witness to others about the Lord, and enabled me to help deliver those oppressed by unclean spirits. I didn't know it was possible for an ordinary Christian to help set people free from evil, tormenting spirits."

- Gloria, who was reared an orthodox Jew, came to Christ after a long period of rebellion against God. Three weeks after her conversion, while reading a book that suggested asking for the baptism of the Holy Spirit, she spontaneously began to speak a phrase in tongues. Her friend and "momma in the Lord" showed her that this occurred in the New Testament during the Jewish Feast of Pentecost, and that her experience was biblical. She kept using her limited prayer language, but a few days later an amazing thing happened.

"Suddenly I broke loose singing in tongues, and it was the most glorious Hebrew pouring from my lips I have ever heard," Gloria reported. She could not speak Hebrew, but she recognized it from years of attending synagogue. "I felt as if I were sitting in the synagogue. My experience of speaking in tongues validated my encounter with Jesus, because all my life I had understood that if one of my people accepted Jesus, he was no longer a Jew. But now for the first time since becoming a believer I knew that I was definitely still a Jew! After that, the Word of God really became alive for me."

The experiences of these women are diverse, yet all of them have several things in common:

1. Each had accepted Christ as Savior prior to her experience with the Holy Spirit (as in Acts 8:15-17).

2. Each felt a need to seek a deeper relationship with the Lord.

3. Each woman's encounter with the Holy Spirit impacted her life according to her individual needs and personality traits.

A Gift for All God's Children

After his resurrection and just before he ascended to heaven, Jesus appeared to his followers and promised that his Father would send them the Holy Spirit. They were to wait in Jerusalem for this to happen. And when the Holy Spirit came they would be "clothed with power." This word *power*—from the same root as the words *dynamo* or *dynamite*—also means strength, ability, or abundance.[2] In other words, the Holy Spirit would empower and equip them to fulfill their assignment to carry the gospel message to the ends of the earth (see Matthew 28:19-20; Acts 1:8).

Women, including Mary the mother of Jesus, were present when the 120 believers experienced the outpouring of the Holy Spirit in the Upper Room (see Acts 1:14). Obviously, Jesus intended this gift for *all believers*, not just the twelve apostles. All of them heard a rushing, mighty wind, saw fire descend from heaven, and began speaking in languages they had never learned (see Acts 2:1-4).

The Apostle Peter explained the phenomena to the astonished crowd that gathered, then declared: "The promise is for you and your children and for all who are far off—for all whom the Lord our God will call" (Acts 2:39).

Church leaders generally agree that this event marks the birth of the Church—the beginning of the Church age. But many also have taught that miraculous signs, such as speaking in tongues or healing, were only for the early Church—that such signs are no longer necessary because we now have the written Word of God.

Due to such teaching, some believers tend to put the Holy Spirit into a neat, theologically comfortable box which dictates limitations on his work. Others grew in churches where the Holy Spirit was rarely mentioned, or where the term "Holy Ghost" left them bewildered.

History, however, records countless instances of hungry believers asking for the gift Jesus promised. They received the Holy Spirit, often with the outward sign of speaking in tongues. They believe they're included in the "all who are far off" group mentioned in Peter's sermon (see Acts 2:39).

Cooperating with the Holy Spirit

Jesus' promise to his followers was: "I will ask the Father, and he will give you another Counselor to be with you forever—the Spirit of truth" (Jn 14:16-17a). This name *Counselor* for the Holy Spirit means "one called to the side of another for help or counsel."[3] It includes the idea of one who gives legal advice.

But just as God does not force this gift upon his children, neither does the Holy Spirit seize full control of all our decisions. He speaks to us when we take the time to listen, and he is faithful to guide us in a variety of ways. But he never totally overrides our free will. We often neglect even to ask the Holy Spirit for help, and when he does try to help us we sometimes choose to ignore his directions.

A few years ago I (Ruthanne) was teaching a Wednesday night session on spiritual warfare at a church about five miles from my home. After the meeting I talked and prayed with several people, and by the time I left the church it was late.

For a few seconds I considered two possible routes for the trip home, then chose the longer one—a route I had driven many times—because it had fewer traffic lights and was faster. About halfway home, as I approached an intersection, I hit a curb in the left-turn lane and blew out the front left tire.

"God, help me!" I cried out, as I maneuvered the car through the left turn and pulled to the right side of the road. I was sitting there in the dark, engine still running, when it dawned on me that this was an empty stretch of road in one of Dallas' highest crime areas. As the reality of my dilemma set in, I prayed, "Lord, I have only two options here—either walk down this dark road to find a telephone, or stay here in the car until someone comes by who will help me. Please show me what to do."

I felt prompted to walk toward the next intersection a few blocks away. After putting the security bar on the steering wheel and locking the car, I crossed the street to walk facing the traffic, praying with every step that God would send a police car my way.

Soon a white van passed going the same direction I was walking. Some distance ahead I watched it turn into an apartment complex, then in a few minutes I saw headlights approaching me from that direction. My heart began pounding when I saw the vehicle slowing down and pulling over to stop.

"Lord, I have to trust you that this person is safe," I prayed.

The tinted window opened a crack and I heard a woman's voice ask, "How can I help you?" I quickly explained my problem. Then the door of the van opened.

"Get in this car—it's dangerous out there!" the woman said. Great relief swept over me when I saw a Bible lying on the floor of the van as I climbed into the passenger seat and gave my rescuer directions to my home.

"I saw you and your disabled car and prayed for you when I passed a minute ago," she said. "I'm on my way home from church, too. I usually don't take this route home, but I did tonight, and the Lord told me to stop and help you. I pulled into that apartment complex to pray and make sure I heard right."

"Well, I'm very glad you not only heard right, but you obeyed the Lord!" I exclaimed.

Because it was so late, and my husband and I didn't have a second vehicle, we waited until morning to try to retrieve the car—only to discover that thieves had tried to steal it. Thank God I was not helplessly sitting in it when they arrived! The security bar had kept them from driving away, but they vandalized the car and stole all its contents. Police had it towed to the city car pound, where we finally located it.

Our insurance covered the repair costs, but among the items stolen was my well-worn teaching Bible, several copies of my books, and money from that night's book sales. Losing my irreplaceable Bible full of notes was a high price to pay to learn a lesson about heeding the Holy Spirit's gentle nudges.

Looking back on the episode, I wish I had stopped and prayed for direction the moment I felt a slight hesitancy about which route to take. But despite my inattention, the Holy Spirit was faithful to guide the woman in the van to help me. Her obedience possibly kept me from ending up as another statistic in the Dallas crime records.

Receiving God's Abundance

How ironic that believers so often neglect—through ignorance, carelessness, pride, or stubbornness—to avail themselves of the help of the Holy Spirit. They may have just enough spiritual food to survive, but they have no abundance of love, joy, peace, power, and provision in their lives. Others may have had an encounter with the Holy Spirit, but for various reasons failed to keep walking in a deeper revelation of the experience.

Our friend Kerry was reared in a Christian home and educated at several different Christian colleges. Once, while a student—more out of curiosity than spiritual hunger—she allowed an evangelist to pray for her to receive the Holy Spirit. Nothing spectacular happened then, but two days later while lying in bed praying, she suddenly realized she was no longer praying in English, but in tongues.

"I prayed like that for three hours, and I never felt better in my life," Kerry said. "But I had no teaching on the Holy Spirit, and I didn't truly understand what had happened to me. I didn't know I could speak in tongues at will, and so for the next eighteen years, I never used my prayer language."

Kerry's attitude was like that of people who say, "If God wants me to speak in tongues he'll have to do it to me or through me—I'm not going to initiate it."

Years later, at a church camp, a counselor asked her, "Do you speak in tongues?" Kerry related the experience she'd had in college. "But when you speak in tongues, you're still in control," the counselor explained. "So you can pray in tongues whenever you want to." As they prayed together Kerry began speaking in tongues in several different dialects, and the counselor encouraged her to pray like that several times a day.

"After I began doing what the counselor challenged me to do, my discernment was markedly sharpened," Kerry reports. "The Holy Spirit reveals things to me about those I'm counseling or praying for. Praying in tongues enables me to intercede for others when I have no natural knowledge of what is going on in their lives. Of course I know the Holy Spirit was with me from the time I received Christ, but this deeper experience has been a wonderful gift in my life."

Pastor Gerald Rowlands insists that receiving a prayer language is not at all difficult, as some are prone to believe. He says:

When you begin to speak in tongues, it will be you who will initiate it. You will speak the words. But the Holy Spirit will give them to you. The Holy Spirit will furnish you with sounds, words, phrases in your mind.

… As you speak them out boldly in faith, the Holy Spirit will increase your vocabulary. The flow of words will increase until rivers begin to flow forth from your innermost being. Determine that when you have breathed in the Holy Spirit, you will follow that by breathing out praise to God. Determine to do it with your voice, but not with your native language. Expect the Holy Ghost to give you a new tongue at that very moment and, by faith, begin to speak forth that new language. Speak out forcefully whatever the Spirit puts into your mind. You may sense your lips beginning to tremble and feel that your mouth is full of strange sounds. Speak them out boldly.

… Once you begin to speak, keep it up. Let it keep flowing. The more it flows, the freer you will become…. Once you have spoken in tongues, as the Spirit gives you utterance, you can then exercise this gift whenever you wish. Paul says, "I *will* pray with the spirit, and I *will* pray with the understanding also" (1 Cor 14:15, KJV, emphasis ours).[4]

The Holy Spirit Heals Depression

Cindy Jacobs was a young student at a denominational college when she read a book on the power of praise. It mentioned the baptism of the Holy Spirit and using your prayer language for praising the Lord.

"I didn't know anyone who spoke in tongues, but I wanted all the gifts that God had for me," Cindy said. "So I prayed, 'Lord, if this is a valid gift from you, I want it. All the sermons I've heard on it say it is of the devil. I don't know if I have to be what people call a "holy-roller" or not—and I'm real scared. But Lord, if it is valid, give me the baptism of the Holy Spirit with tongues.'"

Then Cindy lifted her hands in praise to the Lord—something she had never seen anyone do.

"I felt washed in peace—his presence was so strong," she told us. "Joy burst out of me and I began to sing hymns to familiar tunes, but then I realized I was not singing in English. I wasn't out of control; the Holy Spirit was flowing through me. I asked myself, 'I wonder what I'm saying?' Immediately the interpretation flooded my mind. I was singing praises to God. It was so heavenly and peaceful. I'd never sung that beautifully before—and I sang in at least five different languages."

The next day several students stopped Cindy on campus and said, "You have the fullness of the Holy Spirit—you're different!"

Cindy hadn't told anyone of her experience and was hesitant to say anything for fear of being misunderstood. "Who told you?" Cindy wondered. Obviously these students had been touched by the Holy Spirit also.

One of the ways she was different is that she was cured of depression. She was so full of joy and light, no cloud of despair could stay.

"Now I could tell Jesus everything about my hurts and disappointments and pour it all out while speaking in tongues," Cindy shared. "Even when I couldn't identify what was causing my depression, I'd pray in tongues for a long time, then it would lift. A dramatic change took place within a short time. I remember looking at my hands and saying, 'There is healing in my hands.' That was awesome."

Cindy's father was a denominational pastor, but he never knew that Cindy had spoken in tongues because he died soon after she had this experience. "Once when I was a child he told me he believed that in the end times, people would again speak in tongues," she said.

Now, twenty-four years since that day in a little rented room near the campus, the Lord uses Cindy to bring healing to the nations and reconciliation to the body of Christ through her ministry organization, Generals of Intercession. She has also seen many people physically healed as she has laid hands on them and prayed for God's touch on their bodies.

A Hunger for the Holy Spirit

If you in some way identify with Cindy's or Kerry's experiences, or if you sense a spiritual hunger like Katy did, this book is for you. And these words of Jesus from Scripture are for you:

So I say to you: Ask and it will be given to you; seek and you will find; knock and the door will be opened to you. For everyone who asks receives; he who seeks finds; and to him who knocks, the door will be opened. Which of you fathers, if your son asks for a fish, will give him a snake instead? Or if he asks for an egg, will give him a scorpion? If you then, though you are evil, know how to give good gifts to your children, how much more will your Father in heaven give the Holy Spirit to those who ask him! (Luke 11:9-13)

Perhaps you are reading this book for several reasons: to grow in spiritual understanding, to clear up confusion about the Holy Spirit, to find greater empowering, or to find a way to release the Holy Spirit in your own life.

We hope to clarify what Scripture teaches about the multi-faceted work of this third person of the Trinity. We also desire to cultivate in you a hunger to learn how the Holy Spirit can deepen your relationship with God and enable you to live a more abundant life.

As you read we pray you will experience the presence and the power of the Holy Spirit in a fresh, exciting, and life-changing way.

PRAYER

Lord, thank you for your incredible gift of the Holy Spirit. Forgive me for not giving attention, as I should, to this gift you've provided. I desire to experience your presence and to know you more intimately, and to sense your unconditional love. Thank you that you will reveal yourself to me in this way through the Holy Spirit. Amen.

EXERCISE

1. What is your personal perception of the Holy Spirit?

2. How do you experience the work of the Holy Spirit in your daily life?

3. Make a list of questions you have regarding the Holy Spirit.

4. Use these verses for group discussion:

   Mark 1:8

   Mark 13:11

   Luke 24:49

   Acts 1:8

   Acts 2:4

   Acts 2:38

THREE

Renewal from the Inside Out

Now the Lord is the Spirit, and where the Spirit of the Lord is, there is freedom. And we, who with unveiled faces all reflect the Lord's glory, are being transformed into his likeness with ever-increasing glory, which comes from the Lord, who is the Spirit.

2 Corinthians 3:17-18

As women, our natural tendency is to want to change our circumstances, our husbands, our children, our home decor, and occasionally our hairstyle. But who wants to change on the inside? Or change our way of thinking? Not many of us volunteer for true metamorphosis.

To be renewed—or "transformed," as the Scripture says—means to be *changed* by the work of the Holy Spirit. Not in a cosmetic way, which deals only with the surface, but in a deep and lasting way, which changes our very nature. In a way which causes us to look at life around us differently—as Quin's testimony illustrates.

Initially God made us in his image, but not with his character. Because he created us with a free will, we must daily *choose* to model his character. In the above passage, the Apostle Paul declares that because of his experience with the Holy Spirit, he is being transformed to God's likeness and can live in such a way as to reflect God's character.[1]

The message of this book is that it is possible for all of us. But to be conformed to Christ's image, we must cooperate with the work the Holy Spirit wants to do in us.

Well-known author Catherine Marshall, in her book *The Helper,* relates how her experience with the Holy Spirit gradually changed her from the inside out. Shortly after asking God for this gift, she began to be aware of the Spirit's still, small voice in her heart. When she was about to speak harsh or negative words to someone—or even too many words—she would feel a sharp check on the inside. The Holy Spirit began helping her with daily decisions, and in her witnessing to others of Jesus. She writes:

I soon realized that the baptism of the Holy Spirit was no one-time experience, rather a process that would continue throughout my lifetime. True, there was that initial infilling. But how well I knew that I had not thereby been elevated to instant sainthood. In my humanness, self kept creeping back in, so I needed repeated fillings if I were ever to become the mature person God meant me to be.[2]

Desperate for Help

Beverly is a friend who discovered the renewing power of the Holy Spirit in the midst of her desperation. Though she had been a faithful Christian during childhood and her teens, her college activities crowded the Lord out of her life, especially after she met Tom. Two years later they were married in a church wedding, but they never made room for God in their relationship.

"During those years I still believed in God," Beverly said, "but I had drifted away from him. Soon things began to go wrong with our perfect marriage—though outwardly we were attractive, young, and successful. I discovered my husband had given up on God because of traumas during his childhood, and he was full of repressed anger. My reaction to him was to withdraw and shut down.

"When our first son was born we joined a church, but we were merely going through the motions. I had a good job and the respect of my co-workers, but I was miserable. Four years later our second son was born, but by this time I was in a state of chronic depression, was drinking heavily, and suffered with migraine headaches. I wouldn't open the curtains or venture outside unless I had to, and I almost never answered the telephone or the doorbell. Despite having two perfect children, I couldn't shake my depression."

Meanwhile, Tom began having fits of rage, after which he wouldn't speak to Beverly for days. As he heaped blame upon her for their problems, she became more depressed and he became suicidal. Though they were church members during this time and Tom was in a leadership position, it seemed the ministry of the church left them unchanged.

Renewal and Restoration

But within the church was a small group of people who had received the baptism of the Holy Spirit. They began reaching out to Beverly and Tom because, in prayer, they discerned that this young couple had serious problems. One day when a woman in the group phoned, Beverly was suffering with a migraine and agreed to let her come by the house to pray. After prayer Beverly sensed God's peace, and her headache receded.

Then the lady told her about the baptism of the Holy Spirit, and how this would enable her to use a new prayer language to talk to God—using this scripture to explain:

> In the same way, the Spirit helps us in our weakness. We do not know what we ought to pray, but the Spirit himself intercedes for us with groans that words cannot express.
>
> (Romans 8:26)

"Amazingly, that was the only scripture verse I had ever underlined in my Bible as a child," Beverly reported. "Since I always kept my problems to myself, I was delighted with the idea of being able to talk directly to God like that—and I knew I needed to get close to him again. That night I knelt alone beside my bed and silently told God that if he had something more for me, I wanted it. When I opened my mouth to speak, this beautiful language came out. I knew I was talking to God. It seemed his presence enveloped me, and my headache and depression lifted instantly."

That was the beginning of Beverly's renewal from the inside out. A local pastor counseled her and began teaching her truths concerning the Holy Spirit. Two weeks later she found the courage to tell Tom what had happened, only to discover that he had experienced the same thing but had been afraid to tell her. Today, with a restored marriage, they minister to the homeless people in their community through a distribution center which the Lord helped them obtain.

"Our intensive study of God's Word was like massive doses of radiation that healed and restored us, and now we want to help bring hope and restoration to others," Beverly reports. "Of course the enemy has tried to draw me back into depression and sickness—he always tests a victory. But I've found that by regularly staying in the Word and praying in the Spirit, I'm strengthened to stand against these attacks. Also, through the Word and during my prayer times, the Holy Spirit reveals any area in my life that is unpleasing to the Lord."

Body, Soul, and Spirit

It's usually the outward, visible things which we tend to concentrate on changing. We know, of course, there's more to life than things we see with our physical eyes, but usually the intangibles are far down on our priority lists.

Scripture teaches that we consist of three parts: spirit, soul, and body. Only one of the three is actually visible. But the following verse makes it clear that all three are important to God:

May God himself, the God of peace, sanctify you through and through. May your whole spirit, soul and body be kept blameless at the coming of our Lord Jesus Christ (1 Thessalonians 5:23).

The Holy Spirit wants to work in our lives at each of these three levels—spirit, soul, and body—but it must begin with the area of the soul—our mind, emotions, and will. And our will must take the lead. When we *decide* to yield our will to God's will, our thoughts and emotions will follow. This allows the Holy Spirit to reveal—through the spirit part of our being—the areas where attitudes and behavior need changing.

Some believers make the mistake of excusing fleshly sins and weaknesses by claiming that salvation is only for the spirit, not the body. Others go to the opposite extreme—trying through their own strength to attain perfect behavior, feeling they can thus earn their salvation. Both approaches are wrong. God's Word gives clear instruction:

> ... If you live according to the sinful nature, you will die; but if by the Spirit you put to death the misdeeds of the body, you will live, because those who are led by the Spirit of God are sons [and daughters] of God. (Romans 8:13-14)

Entering into true Spirit-filled living requires genuine repentance and turning from sin. Evangelist Charles Finney wrote:

> To one who truly repents, sin looks like a very different thing from what it did before repentance. Instead of being desirable or fascinating, sin now looks the very opposite: most odious and detestable. A truly repentant sinner will be astonished that he could ever have desired sin.
> ... If your repentance is genuine, there is in your mind a conscious change of views and feelings in regard to sin. You are just as conscious of this as you are of a change of views on any other subject.
> ... When repentance is genuine, the disposition to repeat sin is gone. If you have truly repented, you do not now love sin. Now, you do not abstain from sin through fear of punishment, but because you hate it.[3]

Willing to Change

To allow the Holy Spirit to guide me, and to cooperate with his work of changing me from the inside out, requires two things: first, I must acknowledge my own inability to be good enough to earn God's acceptance; second, instead of making excuses for them, I must renounce the areas of weakness and sin which impede my progress toward Spirit-filled living.

We cannot, in our own power, deal a death blow to all our wrong attitudes and misdeeds. Our innate selfish inclination to yield to fleshly desires is continually at war with Spirit-filled living. But when we determine that we truly want to overcome these faults, the Holy Spirit strengthens and enables us to begin the process of changing from the inside out. By his power we can experience transformation.

A Painful Search

Sarah's search for the fullness and renewal of the Holy Spirit took her through painful experiences, but in the process she developed a deep relationship with the Lord. At age twenty-six she heard the gospel for the first time and immediately responded by giving her life to Christ.

"Having grown up with no Christian influence, I now began attending church and delved into all the Bible teachings I could find," she said. "It was living, healing water to my soul. As I learned to pray, I continually asked God to fill me with his Spirit, not really understanding what that meant. Yet I continued walking in my own strength."

Feeling drawn to a deeper intimacy with the Lord, she began attending a charismatic church and entered into the vibrant, God-focused worship. As Sarah continued asking the Lord for the gifts of the Spirit, a new revelation dawned upon her. While she knew how to be nice and polite, the Lord showed her that the fruit of love was not working in her life.

Building a Foundation of Love

"I didn't know how, and wasn't sure I was even willing, to love everyone—especially those in the church who had misunderstood and rejected me, and family members who had hurt me over the years. But for three years I kept asking God to produce this fruit in my character.

"One day my husband, Ted, came home from work tired and irritable. I was upset with him over an earlier dispute and wanted to thrash things out, but he refused and went on to bed. I cried out to the Lord, asking him to let me feel his love and comfort."

But instead of comfort, as Sarah read her Bible she sensed the Lord's rebuke about her attitude toward Ted. These verses especially spoke to her:

I...beg you to reinstate him in your affections *and* assure him in your love for him; For this is my purpose...to test your attitude *and* see if you would stand the test, whether you are obedient *and* altogether agreeable [to following my orders] in everything....To keep Satan from getting the advantage... for we are not ignorant of his wiles *and* intentions. (2 Corinthians 2:8-9,11 TAB)

"It took a few hours that night for me to become broken before the Lord and truly yield to his Lordship," Sarah reported. "But I finally did, because I wanted to obey him more than I wanted my comfort. The next morning I behaved lovingly toward Ted, instead of giving him the silent treatment as I normally would have done. He just took it in stride, but that was OK because I knew I was pleasing the Lord."

Sarah then made a project of following the example she found in the Proverbs 31 woman: "She will comfort, encourage, *and* do him [her husband] only good as long as there is life within her." (v. 12 TAB).

"I studied the definitions of these three words—comfort, encourage, and goodness—and determined to be a doer of the Word," she reported. "The more I practiced this, the easier it became. Over a period of time the Lord enabled me to forgive and release from my judgment anyone I had a grievance against, in obedience to Luke 6:27-38. At last, freedom from more than twenty years of unforgiveness, bitterness, and a broken heart full of pain! Now I could love these people with his love."

As Sarah learned to yield to the Holy Spirit rather than give in to insecurity or fear, she began receiving words of knowledge and words of wisdom for women who would come to her for prayer. Her boldness increased. On occasion she spoke words of prophecy. After several years she received the gift of tongues. But always she prayed the gifts would operate through her with God's love.

"I can't pinpoint a time when I was 'baptized in the Holy Spirit,'" Sarah said. "The more I allowed the Lord to break me and cultivate love in my life, the more the gifts of the Spirit would flow. Luke 3:16 says that Jesus 'will baptize you with the Holy Spirit and with fire.' I believe my baptism of the Holy Spirit took place through being purified through his fire. The important thing was to yield to his will in the area of forgiveness and love, so that I could be renewed from within."

Identify the Hindrances

Part of the process of being renewed from the inside out is to identify the hindrances, as Sarah allowed the Lord to do for her. We often want to change our circumstances or change those close to us—but this keeps us distracted from looking at areas in our own lives which we need to submit to the Holy Spirit for change. Have you allowed anger, bitterness, envy, or alienation to keep you from God's purpose? Are you disappointed with yourself? Disillusioned with God?

If you are suffering due to rejection, abandonment, or

betrayal, remember the Lord Jesus knew what it was like to be betrayed by those close to him. He can identify with your hurts and wounds. When he hung on the cross, bleeding and dying of wounds he didn't deserve, he asked God to forgive his offenders. We can ask the Holy Spirit to enable us to forgive each person who has abused, rejected, or betrayed us. He is called *the Helper*—but we must ask for his help.

When we fail to forgive, we bind ourselves to that person or situation, and to the continuing pain which results from holding onto the grievance. It shows in our faces, in the slump of our shoulders, even in our conversation. Paul wrote:

> Get rid of all bitterness, rage, anger and brawling and slander, along with every form of malice. Be kind and compassionate to one another, forgiving each other, just as in Christ God forgave you. (Ephesians 4:31-32)

This kind of forgiveness means *to bestow a favor unconditionally, demanding nothing in return.*[4] But when Jesus said, "Forgive, and you will be forgiven" (Lk 6:37b), the word used means: *to release, to set at liberty, as when unchaining someone.*[5] When you choose to forgive, you release that person into God's hands for him to deal with his/her offenses in his own way. But you *unchain* yourself from the offender and from the hurt.

Forgiveness Is a Decision

Actually, forgiveness is a decision on our part—an act of the will, an act of obedience to Christ. Our part is to forgive. God's part is to heal. Some of us need to forgive ourselves—for sins that date way back. If that's your situation, accept Jesus' love and forgiveness right now. Then forgive yourself, and don't let yesterday rob you of today.

When we identify these areas of hurt and disappointment and place them in God's hands, we allow him to begin changing us. When the Holy Spirit is humbling you and doing a new work in your heart, weeping may help to release your pent-up frustrations. Don't be surprised if he fills you with tears—washing over you with floods of his peace and healing. As you yield to the Holy Spirit, his love will begin to radiate through you.

Dutch evangelist Corrie ten Boom's writings provide a clear picture of the tremendous value of yielding to the Holy Spirit:

When we are filled with the Holy Spirit, then another step may be necessary. It is possible that some furniture must be removed from the heart: television, or some books, friendships, personal hobbies; everything that can hinder us from following Jesus Christ. We can clear out still more for Jesus, so that we can give more room to the Holy Spirit. My glove cannot do anything by itself, but when my hand is in the glove, it can do a great deal. It can cook, write and do many things! I know that it is not the glove, but the hand in the glove. When I put only one finger in the glove, then it cannot do anything! So it is with us. We are gloves; the Holy Spirit is the hand which can do everything, but we must give him room right into the outer corners of our lives. Then we can expect that he can do a lot in and through us.[6]

Submitting to the Holy Spirit

Sometimes we unknowingly find our identity in what we do— as wife, mother, church worker, or career woman, rather than in being a child of God. Elizabeth, who had been a professional model from age eighteen to thirty, discovered this the hard way. She received the infilling of the Holy Spirit during the 1960s renewal, but several years later she experienced "major spiritual surgery," as she called it.

While she and an older friend, Marlene, canned apples together one day, they began discussing Elizabeth's walk with the Lord. Suddenly the conversation shifted. "Tell me about your modeling career," Marlene said. As Elizabeth chatted on and on about modeling and her TV show, Marlene stopped her.

"That's it!" Marlene exclaimed. "I've been feeling that something was holding you back in your Christian walk, and that's it—pride in modeling."

Elizabeth put down her paring knife and stared at Marlene with amazement.

"*Pride* is sin in God's eyes, Elizabeth," Marlene told her. "Your identity has been in modeling and in your physical beauty, when it should be in Christ Jesus. He's the one who gives you real identity. But because you've so highly esteemed your career as a model, you've allowed a spirit of pride to come in. If you're willing, let's deal with this pride right now—and any other unholy thing the Lord shows you."

Sitting there at the kitchen table, Elizabeth repented and asked God's forgiveness for her deep-rooted pride.

"When was the last time you cried?" Marlene then asked.

"Oh, so long ago I can't even remember," Elizabeth said, shaking her head.

"Well, you need to cry and allow the Holy Spirit to break you," Marlene insisted. "You will soon!"

Their prayer time continued, and forty-five minutes later Elizabeth began to sob. "I cried and cried, feeling so broken," she remembers. "I believe the Lord was replacing my heart of stone with a heart of flesh so that I'd be able to feel compassion for others when they come to me with emotional wounds. As I wept, I began to see myself as accepted in Christ just as I am—it has nothing to do with accomplishments. What a spiritual turning point for me!"

A Spiritual Make-Over

She was a Spirit-filled, praying wife who regularly attended church and tried to raise her children with a holy awe of God. Yet Elizabeth needed deliverance in an area where she had allowed the enemy a foothold. Pride in her appearance, her performance, her modeling success—all were sinful blocks to her seeing that her true identity is in Christ alone.

Dennis and Rita Bennett, early leaders in the Holy Spirit renewal, offered this caution:

> When a person receives the baptism with the Holy Spirit, it doesn't mean he's "arrived" spiritually.... Don't ever yield to the enemy's temptation to cause you to feel superior; pray for the fruit of humility; it is a good antidote. The baptism with the Holy Spirit is just the beginning of a new dimension in your Christian life, and it is still up to you whether you will grow or regress.[7]

Since allowing the Holy Spirit to do a "spiritual make-over" in her life, the beauty of the Lord shines through Elizabeth in a way that surpasses the physical beauty in which she once took pride. She has since prayed with many young Christian women who have hang-ups in their lives similar to those she faced.

Author and psychiatrist John White addresses this issue in his book *Changing on the Inside:*

> He [Jesus] is willing to show us our helplessness, not only in words, but through our experiences. God may do it the slow way, through the normal circumstances of life, or the fast way, by the illumination of the Holy Spirit. Or he may show us by a combination of the two....
>
> If we ask him, then in one way or another, God will do it. He certainly will. Therefore we tell him that, whether we understand the depths of what we are saying, or not, we acknowledge our helplessness. We ask him in his own time and way to deal with us, and for the present to take our words seriously. When we do that, God begins to move in on us, whether we perceive it or not. Sooner or later we will begin to see. Sooner or later his own nature begins to be infused with ours.
>
> Curiously, when this happens, you do not become less yourself, but more yourself. That strength and beauty which is uniquely yours, planned from before creation, begins to

shine more clearly. You share a family likeness because God is the original source of your being. Once the separation is gone from between you, he can restore what you had lost.[8]

Finding Your Purpose

So often we forget who we are, and to whom we belong.

Measuring ourselves by the world's standard, we may feel we are failures. When I (Quin) gave birth to three children in less than four years, I experienced great frustration with my role of motherhood, though I had desperately wanted children. Sometimes while rocking a feverish baby at night, I felt as if I'd never find time to write again. Like some discouraged women I pray with now, I wondered, "Will I always be just a mommy to crying children with runny noses?"

But after receiving the baptism of the Holy Spirit, I acknowledged that with God's help I could *enjoy* my role as a mother and *enjoy* my precious children. Time would bring another period of life when I'd be free to write again. Rather than demeaning our role of motherhood, we should embrace this season of life and recognize what a high calling it is to rear children to serve the Lord.

My pastor, Dutch Sheets, says, "God has an aim for our lives—a goal, an intention, a designated end. God has ordained a purpose for each of us. He equips us with whatever it takes to accomplish that purpose, but he does not require more than that for which he has equipped us."

The story of Esther in Scripture is an example of a woman whom God equipped to fulfill her purpose. Author Eileen Wallis draws this comparison:

Just as Esther fulfilled God's purpose in her generation, you, too, have been called to be a woman of authority and to fulfill your kingdom destiny.

Perhaps you don't understand what that means for you. Esther didn't fully understand either as she took that first trusting step and obeyed God's call. But her mission unfolded as she walked in submission to God, and she discovered that the beauty of her willing spirit became her greatest asset.[9]

If you are frustrated concerning the season of life you are in, ask: *"Lord, what is your purpose for me right now?"* The Holy Spirit wants to help you identify that focus and purpose. Instead of placing unrealistic expectations upon ourselves, we need only agree with what God's Word says about us. Meditating on the following scriptures (sometimes personalized or paraphrased) will help you stay on track:

God is at work in me to will and work for his good pleasure. (Philippians 2:13)

The LORD will fulfill his purpose for me.... (Psalms 138:8a)

For you created my inmost being; you knit me together in my mother's womb. I praise you because I am fearfully and wonderfully made; your works are wonderful, I know that full well. My frame was not hidden from you when I was made in the secret place. When I was woven together in the depths of the earth, your eyes saw my unformed body. All the days ordained for me were written in your book before one of them came to be. (Psalms 139:13-16)

Now to him who is able to do immeasurably more than all we ask or imagine, according to his power that is at work within us, to him be glory in the church and in Christ Jesus throughout all generations.... (Ephesians 3:20-21)

The Amplified Version of this last scripture includes the truth that not only will God fulfill his purpose for us but will also do "far over *and* above all that we [dare] ask or think—infinitely beyond our highest prayers, desires, thoughts, hopes, or dreams."

Does Change Show on the Outside?

As we seek God's purpose for our lives, we also need to seek his presence. His *presence* changes us on the inside. But because our bodies are temples of the Holy Spirit, his *power* changes us on the outside. And through us, he can change others.

When Moses came down from Mt. Sinai with the two tables of testimony in his hands, he was unaware that the skin of his face shone, sending forth beams like light. All because he'd been in God's presence.

When we spend time in his presence and allow the Holy Spirit to change us inwardly, our outward behavior and appearance will reflect the result. Through our countenance and demeanor we can project a sense of peacefulness that reveals the Holy Spirit's work. Because we are daughters of the King, we actually represent the Lord Jesus everywhere we go. Therefore, we should seek to dress discreetly and appropriately whatever the occasion, reflecting the beauty of our maker.

JoAnne Wallace, author of a book for Christian women, *Dress With Style*, explains why:

> Women are created in the image of God and are His handiwork. It is for this reason, if for no other, that you present yourself in the best way possible and keep this gift—your body—attractive. I do not believe that God's creations should be haggard, drab, or dowdy. Nor do I believe they should appear cheap, tasteless, or immodest. Quite the contrary! God created the beauty of sunsets, daffodils, the splendor of the autumn leaves falling in radiant color—and you. His most lovely creation of all.[10]

When our appearance is unkempt and messy, we project an "I don't care" attitude which hinders our witness for the Lord. We ought to give attention to good hygiene and grooming, yet avoid the opposite extreme of undue pride in our appearance. But at the same time, let's not neglect the matter of inner beauty, as Eileen Wallis reminds:

> Scripture... points out that what is most important in God's eyes is what we look like inside. Expensive clothes won't change us, and neither will hand-me-downs.
>
> But once you're changed on the inside, it's bound to have an influence on the clothes you choose to wear and the way you care for your appearance. Your clothes will all bear a new label: "For His glory." That surely means taking the trouble to be clean, neat, and attractive, and looking like you enjoy being a woman. Purity and modesty, however, will be of more concern than the latest fashion.[11]

Want to discover the real you? Want to experience renewal from the inside out? The Holy Spirit is the best make-over artist you can imagine. But we have to put ourselves in his hands for his gentle operation. As we yield to the Spirit we will find some of our most deeply entrenched sin habits giving way so that we may be conformed to the character of Christ.

This time next year, or even a dozen years from now, you will be able to look back and see that you have truly experienced a beautiful metamorphosis.

PRAYER
Lord, help me daily choose to model your character. I want to be continually transformed into your likeness with ever-increasing glory. Let me be more concerned about pleasing you than wanting to change my circumstances or the people around me. Help me to find my identity in you rather than in what I do or where I live. Holy Spirit, I give you permission to change me from the inside out. Thank you that you will do it with your tender love and in your timing. In Jesus' name, Amen.

EXERCISE

Ask yourself:

1. What hindrances in my life prevent the Holy Spirit from working to bring change? (While identifying the hindrances, also recognize the areas where you are now cooperating with the Holy Spirit.)

2. Can I identify the Lord's purpose for me at this season of my life? How can I more fully cooperate with his purpose?

3. Review this checklist of questions concerning appearance:

What in my outward appearance would attract people to Jesus? What would turn them off? Am I careful that what I wear does not cause lust or disgust? Does my appearance reflect spiritual maturity? Does it honor the Lord? Does the message on my T-shirt have a suggestive meaning? Does it pay homage to a false god? Am I a good steward of the clothes I own? Do I practice good personal hygiene?

Why Speak in Tongues?

I [Paul] thank God that I speak in tongues more than all of you... be eager to prophesy, and do not forbid speaking in tongues.

1 Corinthians 14:18,39

We can never comprehend the Holy Spirit by human reasoning alone, nor can we dictate how and when he will do his work. But we cannot afford to take lightly all that Scripture says about this least-understood third person of the Trinity—God's special gift, the Holy Spirit.

Maybe you are asking, *"How can the Holy Spirit help me, an ordinary woman? Isn't it enough to have Jesus?"*

It was Jesus himself who promised that when he returned to heaven he would ask the Father to send "another Counselor." Then he told his followers to wait in Jerusalem until the Spirit came. Obviously, he foresaw just how much they were going to need the help the Holy Spirit provides.

As mentioned earlier, women were among those followers (see Luke 8:1-3), and they were included in the group which gathered in the Upper Room to wait for the promise: "They all joined together constantly in prayer, along with the women and Mary the mother of Jesus, and his brothers." (Acts 1:14)

We find in Scripture that the Holy Spirit's functions in the life of the yielded believer are many and varied, as this list illustrates.

The Holy Spirit...

- Confirms our salvation: Rom 8:16; 1 Jn 3:24; 4:13
- Gives life: Rom 8:5-11
- Gives joy: Acts 13:52; Rom 14:17
- Gives hope: Rom 15:13; 1 Thes 1:6
- Liberates: Rom 8:1-2
- Gives strength to overcome sin: Rom 8:9-11; Gal 5:16
- Seals our inheritance in Christ: 1 Cor 1:22; Eph 1:13-14
- Speaks through us: Mt 10:19-20
- Teaches: Lk 12:12; Jn 14:26; 1 Cor 2:13
- Comforts: Jn 14:16 (KJV)
- Testifies of Jesus: Jn 15:26; 1 Jn 5:6
- Convicts of sin: Jn 16:7-8
- Speaks and guides: Jn 16:13; Acts 10:19, 16:6; Rom 8:14
- Empowers to witness: Lk 4:14; Acts 1:8; 1 Pt 1:12
- Enables to speak with tongues: Acts 2:4, 19:6
- Strengthens and encourages: Acts 9:31
- Loves through us: Rom 5:5
- Produces righteous fruit: Gal 5:22-23
- Helps us pray: Rom 8:26-27; 1 Cor 14:15
- Helps us worship: Eph 5:18-19; Phil 3:3
- Reveals the things of God: 1 Cor 2:9-10
- Gives spiritual gifts: 1 Cor 12:7-11
- Edifies our spirits: 1 Cor 14:2,4; Eph 3:16; Jude 1:18-20
- Unites believers: Phil 2:1-2; Eph 4:3-4

What an extraordinary gift the Father bestowed upon his children when he sent the Holy Spirit to be our helper! Is it any wonder that Satan tries to minimize the significance of the gift, and divide and confuse the body of Christ concerning it?

God's Perfect Timing

Understanding the *timing* of the Holy Spirit's outpouring helps us to understand God's *purpose* for sending this gift. We can do this by reviewing briefly the final days of Jesus' earthly ministry.

The crucifixion of Christ occurred during the Jewish Feast of Passover. This major feast observed Israel's deliverance from Egypt—when God promised through Moses that every household which sacrificed a lamb and put the blood on its doorposts and lintels, would be protected from the plague of death sent upon the Egyptians (see Exodus 12).

Centuries later, Christ was to be "the Lamb of God, who takes away the sin of the world" (Jn 1:29). It was God's plan, therefore, for this sin sacrifice—the death of Christ—to be offered at Passover.

Exactly fifty days after Passover, in Jewish tradition, came the Feast of Weeks (seven weeks plus a day after Passover)—also called *Pentecost,* meaning "fifty." At this festival the people offered to the Lord the first fruits of wheat harvest—acknowledging God's dominion over their land and their labors. Pentecost also commemorated the giving of the Law at Sinai, which occurred fifty days after the Israelites left Egypt. One commentator observes:

It was on the day of Pentecost that the Holy Spirit was first poured out upon the apostles and the Christian church (Acts 2:1-5). On this occasion, as on the Passover seven weeks before, Judaism was at the same time honored and gloriously superseded by Christianity. The paschal lamb gave place to "Christ our Passover;" and the Jewish feast in memory of the giving of the law, to the gift of the Holy Spirit for "every nation under heaven" (v. 5).[1]

Following the Resurrection, Christ remained on earth for forty days. He then commanded his followers to wait in

Jerusalem for the Holy Spirit to come, as Pentecost was still ten days away. The disciples most likely did not understand the importance of waiting for the Day of Pentecost, just as they did not understand until later the significance of Christ's death occurring at Passover. But they waited in obedience.

Bible scholar Stanley M. Horton comments, "Pentecost with its symbolism of harvest was important in that the purpose of the baptism in the Spirit was power for service, especially in the harvest fields of the world.... For the Church it marked the day when the long-awaited spiritual harvest would begin."[2]

Power to Witness, Pray, and Praise

Jesus obviously intended for the gospel to be proclaimed to all peoples everywhere—not just to the Jews:

> He said to them: " ...you will receive power when the Holy Spirit comes on you; and you will be my witnesses in Jerusalem, and in all Judea and Samaria, and to the ends of the earth." (Acts 1:7-8)

Church growth specialist C. Peter Wagner states:

> The missiological task was clear, and it was magnificently implemented in the book of Acts. But it could not be implemented with human power alone. After three years of personal instruction, Jesus had told his disciples to "tarry ye in the city of Jerusalem, until ye be endued with power from on high" (Lk 24:49). Three years with Jesus himself had only partially equipped them for what was ahead. They needed much more than that to engage in the spiritual warfare necessary to take the Kingdom by force (see Matthew 11:12).[3]

Linda, one of our prayer partners, shared with us about her encounter with the Holy Spirit. She had been a Christian for more than twenty years when she read with new interest what happened in the book of Acts. She asked the Lord to fill her with his Holy Spirit, even though her church taught against such a thing.

"When I received the Holy Spirit my first reaction was to sense an overwhelming love for Jesus Christ and a joy I'd never felt before," Linda reported. "I was aware of a strength I'd never encountered—especially the power to pray. I received a prayer language when I asked for this gift, and my prayer life changed dramatically. Not only do I pray more 'with understanding,' I also pray in tongues almost constantly while doing menial tasks."

Linda is one of many we know who, like Quin, was so hungry for more of God she asked to be baptized in the Holy Spirit despite the fact she knew very little about it. Rather than being a detriment, the experience drew them into a deeper love for Jesus, and enabled them to enter into praise and worship on a higher level than ever before.

J. Rodman Williams says:

> From the Pentecostal narrative [Acts 2:7-11 and 10:44-47] it is apparent that tongues are not ordinary speech, but represent the worship of God in a speech that is other than one's own native language. Hence, speaking in tongues might be called *transcendent praise:* praise that goes beyond ordinary capacity and experience.
>
> ... Ordinary language, even music, may be inadequate to declare the wonder of God's gift.... there may be a speech or language more suitable to the experience of the richness of God's spiritual gift. Humanly speaking, this is impossible, but God through his Spirit may go beyond what has been uttered or sung before and bring forth a new language![4]

A One-Time Outpouring?

Perhaps the most serious misconception about the Holy Spirit is the belief that the baptism (or infilling) of the Holy

Spirit and the manifestation of the gifts are not intended for believers today. This view says the event at Pentecost was a one-time outpouring to bring the Church into existence—and that we've been drawing from that supply ever since.

Dr. Horton refutes such an idea:

> The Church is not a reservoir that received one donation of the Spirit forever.... the baptism in the Spirit is immersion into a relationship with a divine Person, not into a fluid or an influence. It is a relationship that can continue to grow and enlarge. Thus the baptism is only a beginning, but it is like a baptism in that it involves a distinct act of obedience and faith on our part.
>
> ... But the Bible also says it was a filling (Acts 2:4).... We should recognize that baptism is something that happens to individuals. Though all were filled at the same moment on the Day of Pentecost, the filling itself was an individual experience. We should expect, therefore, that Jesus, in view of John the Baptist's prophecy, will continue to baptize in the Holy Spirit as long as believers keep coming to Him to receive.[5]

The Sweet Nearness of God

Historical evidence reveals that the fire of the Holy Spirit was never extinguished throughout the history of the church, though it ebbed very low at times.[6]

During the revivals of the Great Awakening in the eighteenth century, various manifestations were reported by people who were touched by the Holy Spirit. Jonathan Edwards' wife Sarah wrote of a seventeen-day period during the outpouring of the Spirit in 1740 and 1741 when she experienced love, power, and what she called "the sweet nearness of God." Following are excerpts from her husband's *Personal Narrative* in which he quotes Sarah's experiences in her own words:

On January 28 she wrote:

That night was the sweetest night I ever had in my life. I never before, for so long a time together, enjoyed so much of the light, and rest and sweetness of heaven in my soul... with a continual, constant and clear sense of Christ's excellent and transcendent love, of *His nearness to me, and my dearness to Him,* with an inexpressibly sweet calmness of soul in an entire rest in Him...(emphasis ours).

... One evening these words "THE COMFORTER IS COME" were accompanied to my soul with such conscious certainty, and such intense joy, that immediately it took away my strength, and I was falling to the floor; when some of those who were near me caught me and held me up.[7]

Not only did the eighteenth-century "Great Awakening" introduce many believers like Sarah to the reality of the Holy Spirit, it also caused many thousands of unbelievers to receive Christ. It was indeed a time of harvest for the church.

During the following century the "Second Great Awakening" occurred in three phases. First was a strong emphasis on prayer and conviction of sin, followed by an outpouring of the Holy Spirit. Evangelism was the second phase, characterized by the preaching of Charles G. Finney, Walter and Phoebe Palmer, Dwight L. Moody, and others. In the third phase, young people were mobilized for the greatest missionary endeavor the church had seen up to that time.[8]

A New Wave of the Holy Spirit

The turn of this century was marked by the outpouring of the Holy Spirit at Charles F. Parham's Bible school in Topeka, Kansas, when Agnes Ozman, a young woman attending the student prayer meeting, was the first to receive the Holy Spirit. This is an excerpt from her report of the experience:

Like some others, I thought I had received the Baptism in the Holy Ghost at the time of consecration, but when I learned that the Holy Spirit was yet to be poured out in greater fullness, my heart became hungry. At times I longed more for the Holy Spirit to come in than for my necessary food. We were admonished to honor the blood of Jesus Christ and to let it do its work in our hearts, and this brought great peace and victory.

On watchnight we had a blessed service, praying that God's blessing might rest upon us as the new year came in. During the first day of 1901 the presence of the Lord was with us in a marked way, stilling our hearts to wait upon Him for greater things. A spirit of prayer was upon us in the evening. It was nearly eleven o'clock on this first of January that it came into my heart to ask that hands be laid upon me that I might receive the gift of the Holy Ghost. As hands were laid upon my head the Holy Spirit fell upon me, and I began to speak in tongues, glorifying God. I talked several languages. It was as though rivers of living water were proceeding from my innermost being.[9]

Pauline Parham, Charles Parham's daughter-in-law, lives close to me (Ruthanne) in the same apartment complex. She reports that shortly after Agnes Ozman received the Holy Spirit, several others in the same prayer meeting had the experience, and news of the meeting brought journalists from the surrounding area. But the reporters got no satisfactory answers from Miss Ozman, because she could speak and write only Chinese for three days. Mrs. Parham says she was told others in the prayer meeting spoke Zulu, Chinese, and Hindi when they received the Holy Spirit. Later, when Charles Parham himself had the experience, he reportedly spoke fluent German, a language he had never learned.

The Azusa Street revival in Los Angeles led by William Seymour soon followed, and from there the Pentecostal movement spread around the world. Leaders of the movement included numerous women, among them Aimee Semple McPherson. In her autobiography she relates her own experience of receiving the infilling of the Holy Spirit when she was a teenager in 1908, after attending a mission church in her town:

> Jesus was more real and near than the things of earth round about me. The desire to praise and worship and adore Him flamed up within my soul. He was so wonderful, so glorious, and this poor tongue of mine so utterly incapable of finding words with which to praise Him.
>
> My lungs began to fill and heave under the power as the Comforter came in.... Unintelligible sounds as of stammering lips and another tongue, spoken of in Isaiah 28:11, began to issue from my lips.... Then suddenly, out of my innermost being flowed rivers of praise in other tongues as the Spirit gave utterance (Acts 2:4). I knew that he was praising Jesus with glorious language, clothing him with honor and glory which I felt but never could have put into words.[10]

Doubt and Resistance

Aimee's mother, who had studied and taught the Bible for years, objected to her experience and forbade her to return to the mission meetings. Aimee agreed that if her mother could show her in Scripture that this experience was not biblical, or was only for the apostolic era of the Church, that she would never go to the mission again. Aimee left for school and her mother spent the entire day studying the Bible, to the neglect of all her household chores. Finding her still seated at the breakfast table when she returned home that evening, Aimee asked what she had found. Her mother replied:

> "Well, dear, I must admit that of a truth, this is that which was spoken of by the prophet Joel, which should come to pass in the last days!"

She had found... that the prophet Joel (2:28-29) had

clearly prophesied that in these last days there should be a wonderful outpouring of the Holy Spirit, likened unto the latter rain, wherein the sons and daughters... were alike to rejoice in this glorious downpour.[11]

Most believers who embraced the Holy Spirit in those early days were dismissed from their denominational churches, and various leaders established different Pentecostal fellowships. Some so-called "mainstream churches" regarded Pentecostals as being on the outer fringe of Christianity; other groups charged their teachings and practices were of the devil. But nothing could stop the movement's growth.

A Changed Family

The ministry of Maria Woodworth-Etter, another widely known woman evangelist of the early 1900s, had a great impact on the Garlock family. John (Ruthanne's husband) had a grandfather who was a hopeless alcoholic and drug addict. Edmund Garlock's violent temper caused much grief for his family—especially the eldest son, Henry, John's father. Upon hearing about a tent revival Mrs. Woodworth-Etter was conducting in the area, Edmund's wife, Jessie, took action. She had been praying for her husband's salvation; now she added feet to her prayers.

Jessie bought a train ticket to Long Hill, Connecticut, gave it to Edmund, and told him to go to the meeting and not come back home until he was changed.[12] A few days later, Henry was working outside when he heard his father walking up the road, singing loudly. His first thought was, "Dad must be drunk again—I'd better get out of sight or I'll get a beating."

Then Henry realized his father was singing a hymn. Edmund gathered Jessie and the children in the old farm house and told them he had been saved, healed, delivered, and filled with the Holy Spirit. Everything about him was so different that Henry and the others hardly recognized him. But the following months proved Edmund's conversion to be real, and soon every member of the family had been filled with the Holy Spirit.

The Holy Spirit Speaks

A few years later Henry enrolled in Bible school, then in 1920 went as a pioneer missionary to the unevangelized interior of Liberia, West Africa. Many miraculous signs accompanied his ministry there, but one remarkable incident involved speaking in tongues.

He had hired porters to trek to the coast to buy food and supplies for the mission station. But en route one of the porters was captured and severely beaten by an enemy tribe; he faced certain death. Others in the party escaped and brought word to Henry. When he went to rescue the man the tribal leaders, enraged by his interference in their affairs, captured him also. Their obvious intent was to kill and eat both men—which was their way of expressing utter contempt for an enemy. Before killing Henry, however, the witch doctor laid his wand at the captive's feet, indicating he could now speak in his own defense. He tells the story in his own words:

Suddenly, I began to shake. This disturbed me, as I did not want the people to know how frightened I really was. Then I realized the Holy Spirit had come upon me and the words of Jesus in Mark 13:11 came to me: "Take no thought beforehand what ye shall speak... but whatsoever shall be given you in that hour, that speak ye: for it is not ye that speak, but the Holy Ghost."

Now, under the anointing of the Holy Spirit, I stood up. I reached down and picked up the witch doctor's wand which he had laid at my feet. I opened my mouth and began by saying, "Ny lay..." meaning, "Listen to me." And then it happened. The Holy Spirit took complete control of my tongue and vocal organs, and there poured from my lips a torrent of words that I had never learned. I did not know what I said, nor how long I spoke. But when I had finished, silence reigned.[13]

Not only was Henry's life spared, the tribal leaders told him, "We see that your God has power and fights for you. What can we do to atone for mistreating you?" They prepared food for the entire party and provided porters to carry the wounded man back to the village they had come from. Many of Henry's siblings and descendants including his son, John, have been involved in missions and other areas of Christian ministry ever since that time.

Greater Zeal, Deeper Faith

My own father (Ruthanne's), a fairly new Christian and a denominational church member, had his life radically changed in the early 1940s when he attended a Pentecostal revival meeting with some of his co-workers. He received the Holy Spirit and spoke in tongues. But when he told my mother about his experience she said, "I don't want to know anything about it, and I'm not going to any of those meetings with you. Just leave me out of it."

He honored her request, but kept going to the revival meetings as well as to daytime prayer gatherings. Soon she became curious about what went on there to cause Dad to have such an interest in spiritual matters. Shortly thereafter, they both visited a nearby Pentecostal church and Mom went forward to receive the Holy Spirit. Not only was she filled with the Spirit, she also experienced such waves of laughter that her sides were sore the next day.

A major long-term impact the Holy Spirit made upon their lives was to increase their faith level to trust God for physical healing. When my older brother was stricken with spinal meningitis, Dad stayed at his bedside through the night praying for God's healing power to touch him. By the next morning my brother was well. When I was about ten years old I was receiving several shots a week for a severe case of eczema, but it was not getting better. One Sunday night my parents had the pastor anoint me with oil and pray for my healing. Within a week the eczema was gone, never to return.

At age thirteen I received the Holy Spirit one Sunday night in the prayer room at church after a year of diligent seeking— in those days we often had "tarrying meetings" after evening services. From the time of that experience I always had a great desire to serve the Lord in some type of ministry.

Sometimes I would go with my dad when he preached at a revival meeting conducted by one of his co-workers, or when he led a Bible study at the local county jail. My Pentecostal upbringing brought with it much rejection by relatives and peers. I sometimes struggled with certain teachings regarding makeup and dress codes which seemed unnecessarily strict, yet I knew my experience with the Holy Spirit was real and I never wanted to renounce it.

Why Did God Choose Tongues?

In the late 1960s the Holy Spirit "jumped the fence" so to speak, as denominational Christians, both Protestant and Catholic, began receiving the Holy Spirit and speaking in tongues in huge numbers. What has come to be called the "charismatic movement" swelled to a crescendo in the '70s, during which time Quin had her Holy Spirit encounter related in Chapter One. The movement waned somewhat in the '80s, but is now responsible to a large degree for the rapid growth of Christian groups in many nations.

The term "charismatic" is based on the Greek word *charisma,* meaning "a gift of grace," because of the emphasis on the exercise of all the gifts of the Spirit. No matter how maligned or misunderstood it may be, the twentieth-century Holy Spirit renewal has definitely changed the face of Christianity around the world.

The phenomenon of speaking in tongues is a major stumbling block for many who say, "I want the Holy Spirit, but I don't want to speak in tongues. Why did God choose tongues, anyway?"

As noted earlier, our human minds cannot comprehend all God's purposes, for he is sovereign. But Scripture does tell us why God confused the languages in the first place. Evil men—envisioning an empire where they would have total control—began building the tower of Babel. This was God's response:

> The LORD said, "If as one people speaking the same language they have begun to do this, then nothing they plan to do will be impossible for them. Come, let us go down and confuse their language so they will not understand each other." So the LORD scattered them from there over all the earth, and they stopped building the city. That is why it was called Babel—because there the LORD confused the language of the whole world. From there the LORD scattered them over the face of the whole earth. (Genesis 11:6-9)

A noted nineteenth-century Bible teacher writes that in Genesis 11, God confused the languages as an expression of his *judgment*, while in Acts 2 he gave various tongues as an expression of his *grace*. But in Revelation 7, "we see all those tongues gathered round the Lamb in *glory*."[14]

Bible teacher Roberta Hromas, granddaughter of Charles F. Parham, offers this understanding: "When God took his finger of fire and set upon each one of those in the upper room, he wrote a new law of love in their hearts and gave them a new language that superseded the languages he had given at the tower of Babel. Those languages brought confusion and competition. But as we receive this new language of the law of love within us, we need not walk in the confusion or competition of Babel."

Why the Fire?

A common reason given for the "one-time outpouring" view is that the tongues of fire appeared only in the Upper Room, and not at any later incidents of people being filled with the Holy Spirit. But Dr. Horton explains the phenomena of fire from heaven in connection with Old Testament symbolism:

> The Old Testament records a progressive development with regard to worship. First, it was simply at an altar, as with Abraham. Then God commanded His people to build a sanctuary in the wilderness, the tabernacle. Fire from heaven came down upon a sacrifice there to indicate God's acceptance of this new sanctuary. But it happened only once. The next change came when Solomon built a temple. Again, fire came down and consumed the sacrifice, indicating God's acceptance of the sanctuary. But it happened only once.
>
> ...Now the old temple was about to be destroyed. (God allowed a 40-year overlap until A.D.70.)...The Body of believers united together is the temple (sanctuary) for the dwelling of God by His Spirit (see Ephesians 2:21-11; 1 Corinthians 3:16). In addition the bodies of the individual believers are each a temple or sanctuary of the Holy Spirit (1 Corinthians 6:19). The appearance of fire came over the whole group to indicate God's acceptance of the whole Body as a temple. Then it broke up with the single tongue on the head of each to show God's acceptance of the body of each as a temple of the Spirit.
>
> These signs were not part of the Pentecostal baptism or the gift of the Spirit. They were not repeated, just as the fire came only once on each new sanctuary in Old Testament times.[15]

What about Emotionalism?

Some argue against contemporary manifestations of the Holy Spirit, claiming that people too often get caught up in emotional excesses. Of course abuses do occur from time to time. People who receive the Holy Spirit don't become instantly perfect. They are vulnerable to making the mistake of placing too much emphasis on one particular gift, or to falling into error.

But occasional abuses do not warrant discrediting the Holy Spirit's work in the lives of believers today. Christian psychiatrist John White says wisely:

> You can be so afraid of your feelings that you impair your capacity for truth. Scripture rings with the cries of people's hearts, their longings, their fears, their exultations and adorations. We begin to die the moment we refuse to feel. *What we must fear is any carnal or evil source of our feelings, or any tendency to place our faith in our feelings rather than in God's Word* [italics ours].
>
> The antithesis in Scripture is not between feelings and faith, but between sight (having to do with visible external reality) and faith. We say, "Seeing is believing," whereas Scripture teaches us we live by faith, not by sight (see 2 Corinthians 5:7).[16]

Have You Received?

We conclude this chapter with the question of Acts 19:2: "Have you received the Holy Spirit since you believed?" Paul asked this of the believers at Ephesus, and learned they were ignorant about the Holy Spirit. But, "when Paul placed his hands on them, the Holy Spirit came on them, and they spoke in tongues and prophesied" (Acts 19:6).

Many believers deprive themselves of the fullness of the Spirit because they feel the issue is too controversial, or because they're afraid of speaking in tongues. But if Jesus speaks of the Holy Spirit as being a "good gift" (Luke 11:13), why rob yourself of this blessing?

Perhaps you once experienced the reality of the Holy Spirit, but you've grown complacent and lukewarm in your Spirit-filled walk. We challenge you—as Paul did Timothy—to "stir up the gifts that are within you..." (1 Tm 1:6) by praying the prayer which follows.

PRAYER

Thank you, Father, for the wonderful gift of the Holy Spirit. I acknowledge my need to receive this gift in greater measure, and to fully enter into Spirit-filled living. Lord, help me to lay aside my prejudices and preconceived ideas about the work of the Holy Spirit, and to open my heart to all you desire to accomplish in me. I fully yield my will to you to receive your work of grace in my life, in Jesus' name, Amen.

EXERCISE

1. Read the Scripture references at the beginning of this chapter to see for yourself what the Bible says about the Holy Spirit.

2. Make a list of the Holy Spirit's attributes, dividing them into two categories: first, the attributes you have seen manifested in your own life; second, those you have not experienced, but wish to.

3. Read the second chapter of Acts, particularly Peter's sermon where he quotes Joel 2:28-32. What do you feel is the significance of the statement, "I will pour out my Spirit on all people... ?"

FIVE

Cultivating the Fruit of the Spirit

But the fruit of the Spirit is love, joy, peace, patience, kindness, goodness, faithfulness, gentleness and self-control. Against such things there is no law.

Galatians 5:22-23

"Welcome to the Lord's House" reads the sign on the front door of the Florida home of Pastor Peter Lord and his wife, Johnnie. On the beautiful handpainted sign are also different pieces of fruit, each labeled with a fruit of the Spirit named in the above verses.

Johnnie Lord, whose husband calls her "one heaven of a woman," has been exhibiting the fruit of the Holy Spirit in her life for almost forty years. Soon after I (Quin) was renewed by the Holy Spirit, God put Johnnie in my life. She and her pastor husband taught eight couples in our home every Sunday night after church for six years.

It was not so much what Johnnie said, but how she lived her life that greatly influenced me. I never saw her become frustrated, lose her temper, or speak sharply in the many years I knew her. Every morning she arose much earlier than her family to pray and enter into the presence of the Lord.

But Johnnie had not always been like this. Before their fourth wedding anniversary, Johnnie had suffered a nervous breakdown. Her determination to be a "perfect" godly woman, mother, and wife at any price nearly cost her her health. Not that she didn't know the Word of God—she and Peter had met in Bible school. She knew the Scriptures. But she had tried to live a godly life in her own strength, instead of relying upon the Holy Spirit.

All of Him in Me

Slowly she recuperated from her breakdown after undergoing shock treatments and taking medication. One day while visiting her in-laws in Jamaica, she heard a preacher speak one sentence that was to change her life: "When Christ came to live in you, *all of him* came to live in you."

"If that's true, what am I doing in this fix?" Johnnie asked herself.

Then she prayed, "Lord, if what that man said is true—if all of Jesus came into me when I became a believer—let me learn to live like that. Show me how to let his Resurrection power live in and through me."

She returned home and began teaching Sunday school and doing the innumerable things expected of a pastor's wife. One Sunday as she was hurrying to get her two young children fed and dressed for church on time, everything seemed to be going wrong.

"It was one of those chaotic mornings—Richard's button popped off his only good shirt, and Susan lost a shoe," Johnnie related. "I found myself getting uptight, even screaming at them—and I had never screamed like that. I stopped midsentence, leaned on the kitchen counter, and began talking to the Lord. 'I'm going to step aside and let you handle this, Lord. Let me react to this stress as you would.' Peace came over me and the children; my frustration was replaced with his calm and love."

Recently I asked Johnnie about that turn-around day. "His Holy Spirit is the form in which Jesus lives in us," she told me. "He comes to abide in us. I realized that morning that if all of Jesus came into me, he didn't leave any of his characteristics outside. That's what I had to begin to appropriate in my life. But I had to give up my way of doing things. I had to say, 'Lord, I turn you loose and I will let you respond in me. I die to my way of handling things.'"

In the beginning, Johnnie found herself experimenting with this new approach. When she became frustrated she tried to remember to stop and pray, "Lord, you've got to work in this situation—in how I respond, what I say, what I do." Finally, it was no longer an experiment for her, but a way of life.

She rediscovered Romans 6. Almost every verse spoke to her, but especially these:

Do not offer the parts of your body to sin, as instruments of wickedness, but rather offer yourselves to God, as those who have been brought from death to life; and offer the parts of your body to him as instruments of righteousness. For sin shall not be your master, because you are not under law, but under grace. (Romans 6:13-14)

Under grace! What a wonderful umbrella Father God provided for us! Even when we make mistakes, his grace is there to pick us up so the Holy Spirit can teach us his ways.

How Does the Holy Spirit Work in Us?

Many Christian women can probably recite from memory the list of the fruits of the Spirit mentioned in Scripture: *love, joy, peace, patience, kindness, goodness, faithfulness, gentleness, and self control.* These qualities, when present in a woman's life, reflect a deeply satisfying relationship with the Lord—a confidence in his care and provision that generates a serene way of life. Yet many women feel this kind of living eludes them as they measure their own flaws against what they perceive as beautiful fruit in someone else's life.

How can we cooperate with the Holy Spirit's work to cultivate fruit in our lives, ridding us of all the junk that harms us?

First, acknowledge that only the Holy Spirit working through us can produce fruit. Left to our own devices, we produce weeds, thorns, and thistles.

Second, recognize that cultivating fruit is not an event, but a process. Being born into the Kingdom is an event; it happens instantly when you believe in Christ and receive his forgiveness from sin. But becoming a mature, fruit-bearing Christian takes place over time as we resist doing things our own way and yield to the ways of the Holy Spirit.

Jesus gave this instruction to his followers, and we need to heed it also:

Remain in me, and I will remain in you. No branch can bear fruit by itself; it must remain in the vine. Neither can you bear fruit unless you remain in me. I am the vine; you are the branches. If a man remains in me and I in him, he will bear much fruit; apart from me you can do nothing. (John 15:4-5)

Bible commentator Herbert Lockyer reminds us:

The Holy Spirit always produces a nobler standard of work than the flesh. And such an outcome does not come through human power but from a holy Presence pervading the life. The fruit of the Spirit is character rather than conduct— being rather than doing.

... Another aspect of fruit is that it does not exist for its own sake or even for the sake of the tree, but for the support, strength, and refreshment of those who care to gather the fruit. Christ, as the Vine, did not live unto Himself. Himself He did not save. If we live for our own sake, we live in vain.[1]

Life by the Spirit

In stark contrast to the fruit of the Spirit mentioned in Galatians is a list of the "acts of the sinful nature" (Gal 5:19-21), which are called "works of the flesh" in the King James Version. Dr. Gordon Fee mentions that these fifteen items are in four categories:

1. illicit sex (three)
2. illicit worship (two)
3. breakdown in relationships (eight)
4. excesses (two)

None of the lists in Scripture is exhaustive (though it's worth noting that most of the "works of the flesh" mentioned have to do with human relationships). Rather, the idea seems to be to highlight the contrast between the behavior of an unbeliever and the behavior of a believer who is yielded to the Holy Spirit. Dr. Fee observes that "'Works' puts emphasis on human endeavor, 'fruit' on divine empowerment."[2]

Let's compare the lists to see how developing the fruit of the Spirit can help us gain victory over fleshly reactions:

Fruits of the Spirit		Works of the Flesh
Love	overcomes	Hatred, envy
Joy	overcomes	Discord
Peace	overcomes	Factions, jealousy
Patience	overcomes	Fits of rage
Kindness and goodness	overcomes	Selfish ambition
Faithfulness	overcomes	Idolatry, witchcraft
Gentleness	overcomes	Dissension
Self-control	overcomes	Sexual immorality, impurity, drunkenness

Actually, the qualities mentioned as the fruit of the Spirit are character traits which Jesus' life perfectly exemplified. His responses could be described as "moving in the opposite spirit."

Such fruit does not grow in a sheltered greenhouse. It develops and thrives in everyday situations as we allow the Holy Spirit to help us pattern our attitudes and behavior toward others after Jesus' example. Paul mentions these qualities in another passage and emphasizes the importance of forgiveness in our social relationships:

> Therefore, as God's chosen people, holy and dearly loved, clothe yourselves with compassion, kindness, humility, gentleness and patience. Bear with each other and forgive whatever grievances you may have against one another. Forgive as the Lord forgave you. And over all these virtues put on love, which binds them all together in perfect unity. (Colossians 3:12-14)

Choosing to Love and Forgive

Noreen's story is a graphic example of choosing to move in the opposite spirit in the face of grief and devastation. When her 21-year-old son, Gardner, was shot and killed for no apparent reason, and the assailant escaped without being identified, she had an important decision to make. To forgive!

In the aftermath of her tragedy Noreen called on the Lord for comfort and strength to resist anger and bitterness. Then she addressed the enemy aloud: "Satan, I claim the soul of Gardner's murderer for the Kingdom of God. You will not get any glory from my son's death."

At the funeral she asked the pastor to announce, "The family has forgiven whoever killed this young man. Even if the murderer is here today, Gardner's mother wants you to know she offers forgiveness."

Some time later police came to tell Noreen they had arrested her son's best friend from early childhood. The news was even more painful because Noreen and this young man's mother had been close friends. He actually had served as a pallbearer at the funeral, and had heard forgiveness spoken over him.

Noreen went to the preliminary hearing to tell her son's murderer she had forgiven him. So far he has not allowed her to visit him in prison, but she has made it her prayer goal to see him accept Jesus as Lord of his life and find healing through God's forgiveness.

Only by the empowerment of the Holy Spirit is Noreen able to turn her back on bitterness and desire for revenge, as the Scripture declares:

> So I say, live by the Spirit, and you will not gratify the desires of the sinful nature. For the sinful nature desires what is contrary to the Spirit, and the Spirit what is contrary to the sinful nature. They are in conflict with each other, so that you do not do what you want. But if you are led by the Spirit, you are not under law. (Galatians 5:16-18)

Bearing Fruit

Let's look more closely at the fruit of the Spirit.

Love.

How can we love even the unlovable? We can't, but the Holy Spirit in us can. The Scripture says, "… God has poured out his love into our hearts by the Holy Spirit, whom he has given us" (Rom 5:5b). I (Quin) remember times when a friend or family member hurt or disappointed me, I'd cry: "Lord, make Romans 5:5 real in my life. I need help now!" At that moment I didn't sense any "natural" love toward the person because of my hurt feelings. But at those times we can call upon the Holy Spirit to help us love others with the love of God which he pours into us.

Christian love is the fruit of his Spirit working in us, producing loving action toward others. Love seeks the highest good of others, regardless of their behavior. Love is self-giving, without asking anything in return. It's the same unconditional love God expressed for the world by sending his son to pay the debt for our sin.[3]

When we've been offended, it seems natural to pray that the Lord will change the person who is in the wrong. But the Holy Spirit may have a different priority, as Carolyn's story suggests.

"After I was filled with the Holy Spirit I became so dissatisfied with my husband's worldly lifestyle that I began to pray, 'God, change him!' she said. "But one day the Holy Spirit seemed to say, *'Carolyn, ask God to change you. "*

"Although it was difficult at first, I began asking the Lord to do a heart-change in me. I knew I needed the fruit of love in my life. Soon I was aware that my attitude really was changing. Amazingly, I was beginning to respond to Mark with more love. And the kinder I became toward him, the less sharp he was toward me."

Loving Mark in this new way didn't mean that Carolyn allowed him to use her for a doormat. Once when he began berating her and heaping blame on her for something not entirely her fault, she prayed for wisdom. The Holy Spirit prompted her to point out the truth in the matter in a diplomatic way, and to tell Mark he was treating her inappropriately.

"After about an hour he apologized—which truly was a miracle," Carolyn reported. "He hasn't yet become a Christian, but he is more tender toward the things of God and he allows me to sing in the church choir and attend church activities. Only after the Holy Spirit showed me my need for more fruit of the Spirit, and I asked for his help, did our marriage relationship improve."

Joy.

One of the attributes of the Holy Spirit is to bring joy. Even in the midst of difficulties, "...the joy of the LORD is your strength" (Neh 8:10b). How can we find joy like that? Again, Jesus is our example:

> ...let us throw off everything that hinders and the sin that so easily entangles, and let us run with perseverance the race

marked out for us. Let us fix our eyes on Jesus, the author and perfecter of our faith, *who for the joy set before him endured the cross,* scorning its shame, and sat down at the right hand of the throne of God. (Hebrews 12:1-2, italics ours)

Jesus was able to endure great suffering because he knew that to fulfill his purpose on earth would bring great joy. The strength of that vision is what sustained him.

Love and joy are "marks of spiritual power," says author Richard J. Foster. He also reminds us, "The rich inner joy of spiritual power knows sorrow and is acquainted with grief. Joy and anguish often have a symbiotic relationship."[4]

We can ask the Holy Spirit to help us keep focused on our purpose in life, and with that vision in mind sustain our joy even in the midst of adversity. Such joy can cause a genuine "make-over"—both of our inner being and of our outward demeanor.

Peace.

This word describes harmonious relationships between men and between nations; friendliness; freedom from molestation; harmonious relationships between God and man.[5] For the Christian, peace is an inner calmness, a stillness, a quiet abiding and dependence upon the Holy Spirit. The words Jesus spoke to his followers before his death still speak to us today: "Peace I leave with you; my peace I give you. I do not give to you as the world gives. Do not let your hearts be troubled and do not be afraid" (Jn 14:27).

When all around you seems in turmoil, the Lord can give you his peace in the midst of the storm. In fact, peace is much more meaningful when it exists in contrast with the surrounding chaos.

Patience.

The Greek word which is sometimes rendered *patience,* and sometimes *longsuffering,* is "always used in contexts involving one's forbearance toward others," writes Dr. Fee. He adds:

Nowhere else does Paul attribute such forbearance to the direct working of the Spirit; but its appearance here shows that Spirit-empowering is not simply for joy and miracles, but for this much-needed quality of "putting up with" those who need long and patient love and kindness (see Colossians 1:11). This is the antidote to "outbursts of rage" (Gal 5:20) or "provoking one another" (Gal 5:26).[6]

In her book *Queen Take Your Throne*, Eileen Wallis shares her own difficult experience of developing this Christ-like quality of forbearance or patience:

I had to learn this during the extremely trying years I cared for my elderly mother-in-law, whose mind had failed. I felt imprisoned by circumstances beyond my control and was desperate to escape the constant restrictions. My patience dried up completely.

The most difficult thing was giving up my own rights.... A battle raged within my spirit as I longed to be free.... I was looking for freedom through escape, but God wanted me to find freedom in the situation. This liberation began the moment I recognized that my all-wise, all-loving heavenly Father was in control. He was using these circumstances as part of a beauty therapy I hadn't realized I needed. I was able to say, "Okay, Lord. I'll hand over my rights and delight to do Your will."

The situation didn't change. But I did. In that act of submission I had accepted the yoke of Christ, and I could face the trial with a new peace.... Our heavenly Teacher encourages us in our successes and keeps reminding us of the grace available in times of need.[7]

Scripture gives us this promise: "Let us not become weary in doing good, for at the proper time we will reap a harvest if we do not give up" (Gal 6:9). The word *patience* also denotes lenience. When you want to exercise revenge, the Holy Spirit can help you to exercise restraint and be lenient enough to extend forgiveness.

Kindness.

Goodness in action, sweetness of disposition, gentleness in dealing with others, benevolence. "The word describes the ability to act for the welfare of those taxing your patience. The Holy Spirit removes abrasive qualities from the character of one under his control."⁸

Sometimes the fruit of kindness seems more difficult to show toward family members than anyone else. Margaret told us that before she received the Holy Spirit, her expectations of her husband, Eric, were mostly negative. Then a friend who would praise Eric for every little thing he did spent time in their home

"The Holy Spirit began to convict me for my negative expectations," Margaret said, "and gave me the idea of writing down all the good things my husband was doing. As I focused on these things, my negative expectations became less and less. Now I can easily express kindness to Eric, and praise and bless him. The change has produced a much greater measure of peace and love in our home."

Goodness.

This refers to excellence of character and morals; the quality of being good or exemplifying good behavior—closely allied with kindness. Dr. Fee says, "If longsuffering means not to 'chew someone's head off' (see Galatians 5:15), kindness means to find ways actively to show mercy to them, to take a towel and wash basin in hand and wash their feet.... Indeed, goodness does not exist apart from its active, concrete expression."⁹

Faithfulness.

The word speaks of the believer who is trustworthy in the performance of duty; who fulfills his promises; who is loyal. It refers to the quality which enables the believer to "live out his trust in God over the long haul."[10]

God's flawless record of being faithful to us should inspire us always to be faithful to him. The Psalmist proclaimed, "But you, O Lord, are a compassionate and gracious God, slow to anger, abounding in love and faithfulness" (Ps 86:15). And Jesus, our example, was faithful even unto death.

Gentleness (meekness).

This is the most difficult of the nine fruits to translate with a single English word. The concept behind the word means to be submissive to the will of God; to be humble, teachable—not too proud to learn; to be considerate toward others. William Barclay says, "What throws most light on its meaning is that the adjective [form of the word] is used of an animal that has been tamed and brought under control; and so the word speaks of that self-control which Christ alone can give."[11]

Self-Control (temperance).

While the other virtues listed as fruits of the Spirit have to do with community and social relationships, this last one has to do with the inner life of individual believers. The root word means "dominion, power, or strength," and basically means to have one's faculties or energies under control of the will.[12]

This fruit is the antidote for the sexual sins mentioned earlier, as well as the sins of excess such as drunkenness, orgies, etc. Total abstinence or asceticism is not the answer here, for that approach too easily turns into legalism.

Critics sometimes have faulted charismatic believers for teaching that deliverance from demonic spirits easily solves the problems of overeating, drinking, and other addictions. In some cases deliverance may be needed, but to develop the fruit of self-control you must choose to appropriate the Holy Spirit's power to gain control over sinful inclinations. The following story illustrates this truth.

Spiritual Fruit-Bearing

After receiving the baptism of the Holy Spirit, Betty Anne lay on her couch for three days reading *The Living Bible.* "I knew nothing about the Bible, but because of my hunger for truth I devoured the New Testament in an easy-to-understand version," she said. "By the third day I'd concluded that smoking two packs of cigarettes a day was not God's will for me if I am indeed the temple of the Holy Spirit. I asked a friend to pray with me to stop smoking, and after we prayed I never smoked again."

Though she'd tried many times on her own to quit, she always found an excuse to start again. But after prayer, Betty Anne was truly free, and her freedom has lasted twenty-four years. "Was it hard?" you may ask.

"Yes, it was, at first," she said. "I'd have itchy eyes and all kinds of symptoms that would shout, 'Just smoke and they will go away.' But I didn't. I'd say, 'Lord, I'm doing my part by not smoking; you do your part by taking away these awful symptoms.' He was faithful, and I knew I had the strength of the Holy Spirit to stay free."

Not only was the fruit of self-control exhibited in Betty Anne's life, but as she cooperated with the work of the Holy Spirit, the fruit of gentleness and meekness began developing.

"My husband said I smiled all the time, and he'd bring me roses to show his pleasure," she said. "My new behavior was quite a contrast to my days of complaining and nagging him because he'd moved me from a comfortable home to a college campus where we lived in a rented house on considerably less income. But after the baptism of the Holy Spirit, I didn't complain again. The bonus was, seeing the changes in me created a spiritual hunger in him. After my husband received the Holy Spirit we began praying together and ministering to others who came to us for help."

All these characteristics of spiritual fruit-bearing, naturally speaking, may seem to be quite unattainable. One day you may have patience, the next day you blow it. One day you have peace, the next day turmoil. One week you feel inexpressible joy, the next week you don't even remember what joy is like. Why?

Fruit is Developed in Yielding

Could it be that we've not cooperated with the Holy Spirit to change our selfish ways? Or depended on him to mature his fruit in us? We rely instead on our own feelings or the circumstances of life at the moment. This is why we need to ask every day for the Holy Spirit to work in our hearts so that we will bear his fruits and reflect the character of Jesus.

Often our problem is choosing to yield to him. When I (Quin) heard Dr. Peter Wagner tell his Sunday school class, "The fruit is in the root," something clicked for me that morning.

I said to myself, "If the Lord is the vine and I, as a branch, am connected to that vine, then I will produce godly fruit. However, some of my fruit is certainly undeveloped." The words of Jesus teach us these valuable lessons about fruit-bearing:

By their fruit you will recognize them. Do people pick grapes from thornbushes, or figs from thistles? Likewise every good tree bears good fruit, but a bad tree bears bad fruit. A good tree cannot bear bad fruit, and a bad tree cannot bear good fruit.... Thus, by their fruit you will recognize them. (Matthew 7:16-18,20)

I've since come to realize that it takes time and patience for the fruit of the Holy Spirit to grow in my life. Soon after visiting his class, I came across Dr. Wagner's book, *Your Spiritual Gifts Can Help Your Church Grow.* In it he explains:

The fruit of the Spirit is the normal, expected outcome of Christian growth, maturity, holiness, Christlikeness and fullness of the Holy Spirit. Because all Christians have the responsibility of growing in their faith, all have the responsibility of developing the fruit of the Spirit. Fruit is not *discovered* as are the gifts; it is *developed* through the believer's walk with God and through yieldedness to the Holy Spirit. Although spiritual gifts help define what a Christian *does*, the fruit of the Spirit helps define what a Christian *is*.[13]

Guidelines for Godliness

In writing to a young preacher named Titus, the Apostle Paul emphasized the need for godly characteristics among both men and women. He gave guidelines for holiness among the women, and also gave this admonition:

Likewise, teach the older women to be reverent in the way they live, not to be slanderers or addicted to much wine, but to teach what is good. Then they can train the younger women to love their husbands and children, to be self-controlled and pure, to be busy at home, to be kind, and to be subject to their husbands, so that no one will malign the word of God. (Titus 2:3-5)

Older women, then, are to set a proper example for younger women—giving good counsel, teaching what is right, wisely training them in Christian character and homemaking skills. Today we call this principle *mentoring*: the passing down of knowledge and training from one who is more experienced to one who is less experienced.

One woman more experienced in a particular area can teach or train one less experienced, regardless of their respective ages. The goal is to develop the highest potential of the one being trained. While the older women are admonished to do the training, it's often necessary for the younger women to ask for help. That can be humbling.

Sometimes, however, we may be in the process of being mentored even without being aware of it. I (Quin) am eternally grateful for mature Christian women who came into my life to mentor me in different areas and in different seasons of my growth—especially these:

Mary Jo Looney, who taught me that a house could become a haven for my family, even on a shoestring budget. Lib Parker, who mentored me in how to practice hospitality. JoAnne Bailey, who taught me by example how to be at ease in any housing accommodation in countries around the world. Fran Ewing, who modeled how to be specific and disciplined in my prayer life. Margaret Broward, who taught me how to bake bread. Laura Watson, who encouraged me to take myself less seriously. Dee Eastman, who inspired me to trust God's promises for my family even in crisis times.

If you reflect on your own life, no doubt you will recall certain women who have taught you practical and spiritual principles. Have you, on the other hand, had an opportunity to train—or mentor—some younger women?

Modern Day Mentor

Jane Hansen is a very busy woman serving as president of Aglow International, which has ministry outreaches to women in 126 nations. But she was so concerned about the need for younger women to be discipled by older Christian women that she took action. She decided to mentor a group of young women in her own home one night a month. Even though she travels the world she still finds time for her "at-home ministry night."

Jane, a statuesque blonde, is a beautiful woman inside and out. Decorating and baking are her talents, and she has a knack for making you feel at ease the moment you walk into her home in a Seattle suburb. Her serenity draws people to Jesus.

Jane made a guest list of young women she knew who were between the ages of nineteen and thirty-five, including her own daughter. Some were married, some single; some of the married ones had children, as did some of the single women. Some were Christians, some were not; some had been baptized in the Holy Spirit, others had not.

"Although I would provide a setting that was open and safe for the young women to share their hearts, I wanted it to be really special for them," she related. "I wanted each one to feel loved and cared about."

Jane planned and prepared the meal, the decorations, the warm atmosphere, and the sharing time so that each young woman would feel welcomed and accepted. It was to be a fun, festive, and relaxed evening where they didn't even have to cook.

After the first meeting Jane realized some felt uncomfortable when asked to pray or to look up verses in the Bible. To alleviate this embarrassment she brought several simple Bible studies and let them pick the one they'd like to study. The workbook questions provided a springboard for them to share their own needs and concerns.

"We've had some very poignant times when the young women poured out their hurts, fears, and frustrations," she says. "But they have found acceptance, affirmation, and the unconditional love so necessary to the healing process. We've dealt with very real issues such as unfulfilling marriages, unplanned pregnancies, dysfunctional relationships, and the pain these situations cause."

The group also plans evenings when the focus is on practical helps such as homemaking skills, decorating ideas, or make-up tips. For whatever subject the young women seem most interested in, Jane tries to be a helpful teacher.[14]

Others are following Jane's example, as she has shared about her mentoring group that is now three years old. They, too, are finding time to have young women in their homes, asking the Holy Spirit for a format that will work best for their particular group. I (Quin) for one am discipling some single young women from my church. (See end of this chapter for the disciplines I use.)

Biblical Mentoring

In biblical times a daughter often married at an early age and the mother-in-law stepped in to continue the training the girl's own mother had begun. Daughter-in-law and mother-in-law usually developed a deep and continuing bond.

Have you ever imagined the mentoring that went on—woman to woman—in the Bible accounts? Naomi repeatedly referred to her daughter-in-law Ruth as "my daughter" and we know she taught her about spiritual things. Ruth stuck by her when Naomi decided as a widow to return to her Israelite people. "Your people will be my people and your God my God," Ruth told her (Ru 1:16b). Naomi instructed and trained Ruth after their return to Israel. Later, through her marriage to Boaz, Ruth became a part of the lineage of Christ.

Think of the older woman Elizabeth, while pregnant with John the Baptist, mentoring her cousin, the young virgin Mary, who awaited the birth of the Messiah she carried in her womb. These two women relatives rejoiced and praised God for his goodness to them in their time spent together (see Luke 1:35-56).

Lois was a woman who instilled spiritual truths into her daughter Eunice, who had a son named Timothy. Together, grandmother and mother had an impact on this young evangelist whom Paul highly treasured as one who would later carry on his ministry (see 2 Timothy 1:5).

Dorcas, a well-known seamstress, was resurrected after her untimely death through the prayers of Peter, because her ministry was so needed (see Acts 9). Ever thought of all the others she might have mentored—or taught to sew?

The Holy Spirit can teach you through Scripture and encourage you in the stresses of daily life to exhibit the fruit of the Spirit. But when he provides a mentor to speak into your life on a regular basis, the process is easier. And it makes you accountable to someone more mature in the Lord.

We encourage you to cooperate with the Holy Spirit as he

1. convicts you when you need development and maturing in one of the fruits;

2. reveals to you through prayer practical ways to go about it;

3. calls you to become accountable to someone, preferably a mature Christian woman who can help you in your pursuit of a more godly life.

PRAYER

(You may pray this prayer, based on Colossians 1:9-12 and Romans 15:13, for yourself. You can also pray it for someone else by inserting the appropriate name and changing the pronouns.)

Lord, I ask you to fill me with the knowledge of your will and all spiritual wisdom and understanding. Help me to live a life worthy of you, Lord, pleasing you in every way: bearing fruit in every good work, growing in the knowledge of God. Strengthen me with all power according to your glorious might so that I may have great endurance and patience, joyfully giving thanks to you, Father, for you have qualified me to share in the inheritance of the saints in the kingdom of light. Lord, I pray that you, the God of hope, will fill me with all joy and peace as I trust in you, so that I may overflow with hope by the power of the Holy Spirit, Amen.

EXERCISE

1. Ask the Lord to show you which of the fruit of the Spirit you need to focus on cultivating.

2. Ask the Holy Spirit to direct you to one or more capable older women who would be willing to mentor you in areas where you feel weakest.

3. Be prepared to be accountable to them—meeting once a month on a regular basis or communicating by phone or letter.

4. Be willing to take correction without feeling condemnation.

5. Be serious about desiring spiritual change in your life, and

pray regularly for the woman who will be speaking into your life.

Guidelines for Mentoring

When I (Quin) first formed my mentoring group of young single Christian women, I made up the following workbook list, which we used for several months. This helped them to be disciplined and accountable. Our textbook is *A Christian Woman's Guide to Hospitality*, which I wrote with Laura Watson (Servant Publications).

Since "older women are...to encourage the younger women" (Ti 2:3-5) I first set my own goals as a mentor.

- Help the young women discover their life-purpose (see Luke 1:38; Ephesians 2:10).
- Encourage and equip them to live for God's glory.
- Pray for them individually according to needs and goals.
- Include homemaking skills and hospitality helps.
- Get other women to help me when the group has an interest in learning something I am not skilled in doing.
- Answer questions when they arise. If I don't know the answer, find someone who does.
- Let them occasionally reciprocate by planning a meal we can enjoy together at someone's home other than mine.

Workbook Pages For the Young Single Women
I Am Mentoring

1. Write out your life verse from the Bible.
2. Write out your life's goal. Be specific, not "religious."
3. Write out what season you think you are in right now. (You may think *waiting* season or *learning* season, etc.)
4. Write out disappointments or detours en route to your life's goal. How did you handle them?
5. What are you doing right now toward those goals?

6. How do you handle relationships? With other females? With guys? Are you shy? Bold? Overpowering? Do you get hurt and drop friendships over slight misunderstandings?

7. Do you have some close friends your own age that you can pray with on a regular basis?

8. Do you have a problem with worry or anxiety? Or with weight? Whatever your weak area, find at least three Bible verses that speak to that situation and memorize them. (Example: If it is worry, you'd find several times when Jesus said, "Do not be anxious." To worry is a distraction; it is not trusting God to meet your needs).

9. How do other people see you? What image do you portray? Do you have a good self-image or a sloppy don't-care one?

10. Do you want help in some skills you haven't yet developed and if so, have you considered which older woman in our church could help teach you? Example: how to bake bread, apply make-up, or make your bedroom more attractive and less messy.

11. Are you disciplined in your prayer life and Bible reading? Set realistic goals for a devotional time with the Lord.

12. What are some of your priorities right now?

13. Get a separate notebook that only you and God will read and get real honest with your Heavenly Father about these areas in your life.

    a. weaknesses

    b. strengths

    c. wise use of your gifts and talents

    d. ways you have not wisely used those gifts and talents

    e. people you hold grudges against because of past hurts and disappointments. Choose to forgive them so God can unchain (loose) you from that bondage and hear your prayers (see Mark 11:22-26).

SIX

The Gifted Woman
on a Mission

As each one has received a gift, minister it to one another, as
good stewards of the manifold grace of God.

1 Peter 4:10, NKJV

God equips each believer to play a significant role within the body of Christ, which is incredibly varied and diverse. The gifts he has given are a crucial part of your purpose and mission as a daughter of God, but often these gifts are buried under insecurity, fear, doubt, or deception. Or perhaps you've allowed others, through their rejection or discouragement, to squelch the expression of your gifts, causing you to see yourself with distorted vision.

The Holy Spirit desires to free you from any bondages and misconceptions about yourself, so you can receive his revelation concerning the areas of your giftedness. But it requires times of prayer and waiting on the Lord for him to speak and instill vision within you for how you can be a good steward of your gifts.

In exploring the topic of spiritual gifts, we hope you will discover which ones are yours, and how you can more fully develop them along with the fruit of the Spirit.

Our Own Experience

Quin and I (Ruthanne) feel that both of us have gifts in the areas of teaching and exhortation—otherwise we wouldn't be writing books like this one. But discovering those gifts took place over time as we learned through trial and error to depend upon the Holy Spirit, trusting him to help us develop in these areas and overcome feelings of inferiority.

It's all too easy for us to observe someone else operating in a particular gift, and then to feel we're ill-qualified by comparison. I've sometimes felt that way because a few of my friends have such strong prophetic gifts and often give words of knowledge in public meetings—which I almost never do.

Yet upon reflection I remember a time when I was praying for a woman during a church meeting and the Holy Spirit gave me a word of knowledge that she had suffered serious child abuse. I knelt beside her and whispered that in her ear, then laid hands on her and began praying in tongues. She told me later, "I don't know what you were saying when you prayed like that, but I felt a healing was taking place deep in my spirit." I'm still learning simply to allow the Holy Spirit to work through me as he desires—not worrying about measuring up to preconceived expectations, whether my own or someone else's.

Jack Hayford, in his book *Spirit-Filled: The Overflowing Power of the Holy Spirit* emphasizes that all the gifts are available to those who are open to the Holy Spirit:

There is no status among the gifts. But because they are listed in a sequence some people argue that some gifts are more worthy than others. The fruits of the Spirit also are listed in an order, yet no one is foolish enough to suggest one characteristic to be more or less prized or significant than another. Also, you may occasionally hear someone suggest one gift is more desirable than another (example: wisdom), or to refer to "tongues" as "the least of the gifts."

Of course, that isn't scriptural. In fact, that quotation ("least of the gifts") is not in the Bible, but is of human invention.

The Holy Spirit makes the whole spectrum of gifts available to the believer who is wholeheartedly open. So, the way you may receive the gifts of the Holy Spirit is to live in that openness and to exercise them in the spirit of his love.[1]

Who Gives Spiritual Gifts?

We find in Scripture three major passages where spiritual gifts are listed. The context of each list indicates that the gifts in the first group are given by God the Father, those in the second group are given by the Holy Spirit, and those in the third group are given to the church by Christ. The references are:

1. Romans 12:3-8—**Gifts of the Father** (seven). Basic life purpose and motivation gifts for the individual.
2. 1 Corinthians 12:8-10, 28—**Gifts of the Holy Spirit** (nine). To benefit or strengthen the Body of the Church.
3. Ephesians 4:11—**Gifts of the Son** (five). To facilitate and equip the Body of the Church.[2]

In the first passage the writer uses the analogy of a physical body to illustrate the variety of gifts which God gives to individual believers—both men and women—so they can function together as the body of Christ:

For as we have many members in one body, but all the members do not have the same function, so we, being many, are one body in Christ, and individually members of one another.

Having then gifts differing according to the grace that is given to us, let us use them: if prophecy, let us prophesy in proportion to our faith; or ministry, let us use it in our ministering; he who teaches, in teaching; he who exhorts, in exhortation; he who gives, with liberality; he who leads, with diligence; he who shows mercy, with cheerfulness. (Romans 12:4-8, NKJV)

Motivational Gifts

The gifts mentioned in the above passage are often called "motivational gifts," implying that these are inherent tendencies a person is born with because of God's unique workmanship in creating each individual.[3]

We define these gifts as follows:

1. *Prophecy* - To be enabled by the Spirit to speak moral truths with boldness and insight, influencing others to perceive and embrace the truth.

2. *Ministry* - To render loving service to meet the needs of others.

3. *Teaching* - Ability to explain and clarify truths received from God.

4. *Exhortation* - Calling one aside to encourage him/her to pursue some course of conduct in the future.

5. *Giving* - Sharing one's resources with generosity.

6. *Leadership* - Ability to do administrative work in the Body and exercise authority with diligence.

7. *Mercy* - To relate to others with empathy for their problems, exhibiting respect, honesty, kindness, and cheerfulness.[4]

If you're confused as to what your own gifts are, we suggest you write down a personal inventory of those activities in which you find the greatest personal fulfillment. For the most part, you will discover your gifts in those areas. Dr. Wagner gives this insight:

My concept is this. The same God who gives spiritual gifts also oversees the way each one of us is made up in our total being. God knows every detail of our psychological condition, our glands and hormones, our metabolism, our total personality. He understands our feelings perfectly. And he knows that if we enjoy doing a task we do a better job at it than if we do not enjoy it. So part of God's plan, as I understand it, is to match the spiritual gift He gives us with our temperament in such a way that if we really have a gift we will feel good using it.... God reserves the assigning of spiritual gifts to Himself. All the computers at IBM would not be equipped to assign gifts for the hundreds of millions of Christians around the world, but it is no problem to God Almighty.[5]

Many surveys and tests are available from various sources to help you more specifically identify your gifts if you feel the need for that kind of direction.[6] However, as with the fruits of the Spirit mentioned in Chapter Five, we feel one of the best ways to develop confidence in the use of your gifts is to learn by example from those who are more mature in the Spirit.

Author Annie Chapman suggests:

Instead of focusing on uncovering our gift, which can get to be a bit self-centered, I propose we major instead on asking, "What are the needs I see around me? What ideas or skills or possessions do I have to help meet those needs?"

With this kind of focus, we'll worry less about our capabilities, and more about loving and serving. In the process of giving, our "gift" will emerge... if we begin to serve others we'll see where God blesses us and how He uses us best, and our gifts will be obvious to all.[7]

We agree with Annie Chapman that we're happiest when we use our gifts to help meet needs about us. I (Quin) enjoy teaching the young women in our church I'm mentoring much more than cooking a meal to take to a needy family. However, in my younger years I cooked and delivered many, many meals for the sick. Today I'm happiest writing books, speaking to women's groups, and interceding for those God calls me to pray for. One of my heart's desires is to see women set free to be all that God has called them to be.

On the other hand, LeRoy, in this season of his life, uses his gifts of leadership (called *helps* in the KJV) to supervise the

Christmas food basket project, visit the sick, and make pastoral calls at the county jail. Our giftings are very different but we free one another to operate in the areas where we're most productive for the work of the Lord.

Gifts Given by the Spirit

The following passage lists the "nine gifts of the Spirit" as they usually are called—gifts given by the Holy Spirit to members of the body of Christ to help the entire Church:

> Now there are diversities of gifts, but the same Spirit. There are differences of ministries, but the same Lord. And there are diversities of activities, but it is the same God who works all in all. But the manifestation of the Spirit is given to each one for the profit of all: for to one is given the word of wisdom through the Spirit, to another the word of knowledge through the same Spirit, to another faith by the same Spirit, to another gifts of healing by the same Spirit, to another the working of miracles, to another prophecy, to another discerning of spirits, to another different kinds of tongues, to another the interpretation of tongues. But one and the same Spirit works all these things, distributing to each one individually as He wills. For as the body is one and has many members, but all the members of that one body, being many, are one body, so also is Christ. (1 Corinthians 12:4-12, NKJV)

Dr. Fee's well-reasoned view is that this list actually is not exhaustive, but was given by Paul to the Corinthian believers to represent the *diversity* of the Spirit's manifestations to keep them from overemphasizing or abusing the gift of tongues.[8]

Certainly, we shouldn't use this list to label or compartmentalize anyone—including ourselves. Scripture says we should "desire spiritual gifts" (see 1 Corinthians 12:31 and 14:1), and this implies we ought to be open to allowing any of the gifts to work in us as the Holy Spirit sees fit. A spiritual gift is a supernatural ability bestowed on an individual by the Holy Spirit; it is not merely a heightened natural ability.

We agree with Dr. Wagner's observation:

> Many Christians are multigifted.... Probably the majority, or perhaps all Christians, have what we could call a "gift-mix" instead of a single gift.
>
> ... Paul says that the Spirit has distributed the gifts to "each one for the profit of all" (1 Cor 12:7). Most people agree that "each one" includes both women and men. Unfortunately, the King James Version says "to every man" and some still insist that it should be taken literally. It should not. Women, as well as men, are members of the Body and receive spiritual gifts.[9]

Let's explore the meanings of the various gifts mentioned in 1 Corinthians 12, and look at examples of how these gifts operate. Our definitions are taken from the *Spirit-Filled Life Bible:*[10]

Word of wisdom.
A spiritual utterance at a given moment through the Spirit, supernaturally disclosing the mind, purpose and way of God as applied to a specific situation.

Scripture encourages us, when we lack wisdom, to ask for it: "If any of you lacks wisdom, he should ask God, who gives generously to all without finding fault, and it will be given to him" (Jas 1:5). But we must lay aside human wisdom in order to operate in the gift of wisdom. The manifestation of this gift seems much less spectacular than others mentioned, but it is infinitely valuable.

Gordon Lindsay calls the word of wisdom "a fragment of divine wisdom that is given by supernatural means." He goes on to say:

> The word of wisdom is not a development of human or natural wisdom.... One of the most widespread errors is the sup-

position that the word of wisdom is a God-endowed faculty of human wisdom. This is no more true than to suppose that the medical profession represents the gifts of healing.

... One method by which the Lord imparts the word of wisdom is by audible voice [as in 1 Samuel 3].... Undoubtedly there are those who receive the word of wisdom by direct intuition. A certain course of action may seem to the natural senses to be quite logical. But suddenly the person may be stopped in his tracks. Nothing has been said, but the person knows beyond all doubt that God has spoken. Subsequent events prove that the change of plan was the wisest thing that could have happened.[11]

Word of Knowledge.

A supernatural revelation of information pertaining to a person or an event, given for a specific purpose, usually having to do with an immediate need.

Maybe you once met a stranger and just "knew" something about that person without ever really conversing with the individual. God gave you a word of knowledge—a supernatural revelation pertaining to that person for a specific intent. This could have been simply for you to pray more specifically for that person, or perhaps for you to encourage him or her.

On the night I (Quin) asked Pastor Mobley to pray for me to be filled with the Holy Spirit, he received a word of knowledge about me. "Before I pray for you to receive the Holy Spirit, I need to ask you a question," he said. "Who is it that you need to forgive?"

His question surprised me, but I knew immediately who it was. "My father," I answered. The pastor did not know that my dad had deserted our family—Mom and four of us children— for his secretary when I was twelve years old. Though I hadn't been consciously aware of it through all those years, I had a deeply-buried resentment against him for the hardship his choice had caused all of us.

Pastor Mobley showed me in Mark 11:25-26 that to forgive was a condition for having my prayers answered, and for receiving God's forgiveness. Though I didn't want to forgive Daddy, and I certainly didn't feel like it, I had no choice if I wanted God to answer my prayers. My will and emotions had to yield to the Holy Spirit.

So I prayed, "God, I choose to forgive Daddy for abandoning me. Please forgive me for all the hate, anger, bitterness, and malice I've harbored in my heart all these years. Lord, I now receive your forgiveness."

Then I was ready to pray to receive the baptism of the Holy Spirit. The Lord not only answered my prayer by baptizing me with his Spirit, he also gave me a baptism of love for my father. After all those years of silence, I began writing him letters to reestablish our relationship.

Until that night in the pastor's study, I never knew that such a thing as a word of knowledge was a gift of the Spirit available to all believers. I have since experienced the Holy Spirit giving me words of knowledge as I pray for others. When this happens, it always confirms to an individual that God knows her heart and cares about her needs.

The Gift of Faith.
A unique form of faith that goes beyond natural faith and saving faith. It supernaturally trusts and does not doubt with reference to the specific matters involved.

Ruth E. Garlock (Ruthanne's mother-in-law) faced a desperate situation as a twenty-six-year-old missionary in Liberia, West Africa, in the early 1920s with her husband, Henry. Having had their diet reduced to almost nothing except boiled rice, Ruth became critically malnourished when her system could no longer digest the rice.

Because he had only enough money for one ticket, Henry sent her alone on a freight ship to the Canary Islands, where a doctor told her her only hope of survival was to have stomach surgery. But Ruth chose to trust God for healing, rather than risk surgery under uncertain conditions in a country where she couldn't speak the language. The Spanish maid of an American missionary did her best to take care of her, but Ruth grew weaker, became partially blind, and was soon bedfast. Yet she continued to believe that God would intervene. She tells the story in her own words:

> I had been unable to read for several weeks, but I kept my Bible under my pillow. Occasionally I would thumb the pages, hold it close to me, and pray. One day I felt a special urge to look at my Bible, so I pulled it out from under the pillow and it fell open. All the print was doubled, or blurred, or blanked out, except for the last four words on one page: *"Have faith in God"* (Mark 11:22). Those words stood out in large, clear, bold, black print. As I pondered the words and marveled at the miracle that I could read them, I caught sight of something else. To my right and just above my line of vision quite a distance away, I saw what looked like a black brick. It was iridescent and shining, with marbled streaks of gold in it, and it was moving rapidly toward me. When it reached my chest it vanished, but I knew it was God's gift of faith to me. The experience filled me with an instant assurance that I was healed.
>
> I sat up in bed and began to praise God for healing. Then I slipped out of bed and knelt on the floor, praying and crying and praising God and speaking in tongues. God had touched me and I knew it. After a bit, I rose to get back into bed, and became so sick, so very sick. I knew that this was the crisis moment. If I didn't hold my healing now, I was gone. So I had it out with the devil. "Old devil, this is the last time you can make me sick," I declared. "I am healed. The Word says I am healed, God says I'm healed, the Spirit witnesses that I am healed, and *I am healed!*"[12]

Indeed she was healed. Henry soon joined her, then they traveled by ship to England and on to the United States where their son (Ruthanne's husband) was born a few months later. "The doctor who wanted to operate thought I was crazy when I told him I was pregnant," Mom Garlock said, reflecting on the incident. "But I knew I was going to have a son and that he would be a preacher. I named him John before he was born." At this writing, Mom Garlock is ninety-eight years old and living in a nursing home. Son John has been preaching for more than fifty years.

Gifts of healings.
  Those healings that God performs supernaturally by the Spirit. The plural suggests that as there are many sicknesses and diseases, the gift is related to healings of many disorders.

We believe God can work through the medical profession to cure illness, but we also believe in supernatural healing such as Jesus and his followers practiced in the New Testament. Carol Cartwright, who herself was miraculously healed of mental illness, recently told us of a young woman, Sherry, who came for prayer in one of her meetings. She had just learned that the cancer she thought had been cured was back in her lungs. Through her tears, but without giving details, she told Carol, "The doctors say the cancer I had three years ago is back, and I feel I have too much to do for the Lord to go now."

At first Carol prayed what she calls "soaking prayers" over the woman, releasing God's peace into her troubled spirit. When she placed her hand on the woman's chest, Sherry said, "You've just touched the place where the cancer is." Carol then felt led by the Spirit to take authority over demonic spirits. "Devil, she has been redeemed from the curse of tumors and boils [see Deuteronomy 28:15,27] by the power of Jesus Christ," she declared. "You foul spirit of cancer, loose her body in Jesus' name."

Sherry went back to the doctor that week and they ran tests again. "We don't understand this," her doctor reported to her, "but there's no sign of cancer here."

This is a fulfillment of Jesus' words:

And these signs will accompany those who believe: In my name they will drive out demons;... they will place their hands on sick people, and they will get well. (Mark 16:17a,18b)

Working of Miracles.

A manifestation of power beyond the ordinary course of natural law. It is a divine enablement to do something that could not be done naturally.

Scripture records that "God anointed Jesus of Nazareth with the Holy Spirit and power, and... he went around doing good and healing all who were under the power of the devil, because God was with him" (Acts 10:38).

Smith Wigglesworth, a British evangelist who ministered in the 1930s and 1940s, taught that God wants the believer today to have that same anointing and power. In his own meetings spectacular miracles often occurred. He said:

We must expect God to come forth in power through us for the deliverance of others.... In the former days the prophets received the Holy Spirit in a certain measure, but the Holy Spirit was given to the Lord Jesus Christ without measure. Did not he give the Holy Spirit on the day of Pentecost in this same measure? This is his thought for you and me.

... Faith in God will bring the operation of the Spirit and we will have the divine power flooding the human vessel flowing out in blessing to others.[13]

Once after I (Quin) had addressed a women's meeting, a woman who hadn't spoken a word for more than a year came for prayer. A neighbor who had brought her explained the circumstances. Truthfully, I wasn't sure what to do, having never encountered anything like this before. I silently asked the Holy Spirit to lead me.

First I put my hands on her head and addressed the enemy: "Foul spirit of infirmity, I come against you in the name of Jesus

Christ of Nazareth. Loose your hold on her. You dumb spirit, leave her in Jesus' name."

Looking directly at her, I instructed, "Say 'Jesus.' Say 'Jesus.'"

At first she stuttered, "Je... Je... Je..." Finally she repeated "Jesus" very slowly, then she said it more clearly.

I asked whether she knew Jesus as her personal Savior and Lord. No, she was not a believer. But in regaining her speech and speaking his name with her first words, she had acknowledged him. We then shared the gospel with her, and she received Christ as her Savior and Lord.

Prophecy.

A divine disclosure on behalf of the Spirit, an edifying revelation of the Spirit for the moment (see 1 Corinthians 14:3), a sudden insight of the Spirit, prompting exhortation or comfort (14:30).

In ordinary conversation, "prophecy" means, to most people, a prediction of future events. But in the Bible the word has a much broader, richer meaning. Prophecy consists of speaking *for* God *to* people a message he wants communicated. It is directed to a specific person or persons for a specific purpose, usually at a specific time. As several Bible teachers have put it, "Prophecy is not necessarily *foretelling*, but *forthtelling* what God wants people to hear." The one who gives forth such a message is functioning as a prophet, though he or she may not have (nor need) any official recognition as such.

The gift of prophecy is unique because it's mentioned in all three different groupings of gifts in the Scripture. In addition to the above explanations, prophecy is also considered to be the systematic preaching of the Word. Those who do not acknowledge that all nine gifts still function in the church today believe, in fact, that preaching the Word is *equivalent* to prophecy (based on 1 Corinthians 13:9-10). But we feel this limited interpretation stifles the operation of Spirit-led prophecy in the church.

While we should not give prophetic words spoken in the body of Christ today the same weight as the written Word of

God, we definitely believe the Holy Spirit still speaks through prophetic utterances. Such a prophetic word may be for a single individual, for a specific group or ministry, a congregation, a city, or even for a nation.

Putting a word "on the shelf." Shortly after Mom's death I (Quin) went to Germany to visit her prayer partner whose husband was stationed there. She took me to an Aglow conference where Beth Alves, known for her prophetic ministry, was keynote speaker. I hadn't seen Beth for several years, and she knew little of what was going on in my life, except that Mom had died.

During the first night's meeting—before we'd had a chance to visit—Beth called me forward and spoke a prophetic word to me. I was emotionally and spiritually exhausted after being Mom's caregiver for so long and had come to this conference for spiritual renewal—but certainly didn't expect a prophetic word.

"The Lord wants you to know he was building compassion in you while you cared for your mom," Beth said. "The time wasn't wasted. You will write again—books that will bless many and will be translated into other languages. The Lord wants to encourage you tonight."

My response was to cry and say, "Lord, how can this be?" In this case, her prophecy was not a confirmation to me—it seemed totally impossible. So I left it "on the shelf" and asked God to bring it to pass in his timing.

Within weeks after I returned from Germany, a publisher called and asked me to write a book on how to pray for children. To date it is in five or six languages. Since then seven more books have been written, and several of those also have been translated into other languages. Time proved the word to be true, but it happened in God's timing, not mine.

Space does not allow a thorough discussion of prophecy, but we agree with Paul's word to the Corinthians: "Therefore, my brothers [and sisters], be eager to prophesy, and do not forbid speaking in tongues. But everything should be done in a fitting and orderly way" (1 Cor 14:39-40).

How can I be sure? You may sense the stirring of the Holy Spirit and feel you're receiving a word of prophecy in a given situation. What do you do? How can you be sure you're hearing accurately? How do you begin? In her book, *The Voice of God*, our friend Cindy Jacobs says:

> ... One of the most frequent ways I receive a prophetic word is by simply opening my mouth, starting to speak and trusting the Lord to give me His words.... Other times I receive just a few words or a complete sentence. If I am faithful to share the little portion I have, more of the prophecy comes to me through the inspiration of the Holy Spirit as I go along. On some occasions, I receive the theme of the word and begin with that.
> ... I always encourage people to ask the Lord to allow them to prophesy. Even if they don't have the gift, the Lord may use them occasionally.
> ... So how do you know if and when to prophesy? You can trust the Holy Spirit to give you a deep sense of his presence and peace. One question to ask yourself is, "Is this a prophetic word God is speaking to me personally or is it to be shared with everyone?" Sometimes it can be for both.... Another way to know whether or not to prophesy is to ask an elder what he or she thinks. Mature leaders are usually able to tell whom the presence of the Lord is upon and know that a certain person is the one to give a prophetic word.[14]

Gordon Lindsay wisely says:

> Those who hear a prophecy that seems out of line are not necessarily called upon to judge it publicly nor to set themselves on record about it. There are times when it is wise to keep one's own counsel. However, this does not mean they are to accept blindly all that they hear. While we are not to

despise prophesying, we have the right to compare it with the Scriptures and to "prove all things" and to "hold fast that which is good" (see 1 Thessalonians 5:21).[15]

Discerning of Spirits.
The ability to discern the spirit world, and especially to detect the true source of circumstances or motives of people.

The term *to discern* comes from a Greek root meaning to discriminate, distinguish, or separate.[16] To discern the truth means to separate that which is true from that which is false. Bible teacher Dr. Fuchsia Pickett gives a more thorough explanation:

> The discerning of spirits is not keen mental penetration or the revelation of people's character or thoughts as through a kind of mental telepathy. It is not psychological insight, nor the critical ability to discover faults in others. Neither is it a supernatural power that operates by the will of man, for all God-given spiritual gifts operate only through the will of the Holy Spirit. There are supernatural powers that operate through the will of man. Such forces as clairvoyance, hypnotism, magic, witchcraft, cultism, sorcery, and spiritualism, though real supernatural forces, are satanic in their origin and operate through the perverted will of man.
>
> The Scriptures indicate quite clearly that the gift of discerning of spirits is the God-given ability to discern the source of a spiritual manifestation, whether it is the Holy Spirit, an evil spirit, or merely the human spirit.[17]

Discernment thwarts curses. A minister friend of ours, Carla, was in Canada sitting on the platform of a church where she was the guest speaker, when three women came in late and sat at the back. "Immediately I sensed they were up to no good, and began praying under my breath while the meeting was under way," she said. "When the Holy Spirit showed me they were involved in the occult and were there to try to put curses on me and the church, I began binding demonic spirits and declaring the protection of the blood of Jesus."

It so happened that her message that night was on the gifts of the Holy Spirit, so as Carla preached she talked about the power of God being greater than that of Satan's counterfeits, and stated that the church needs to walk in the Holy Spirit's power once again.

"I was asking the Lord for direction as I was about to invite people to come forward for ministry. I felt he told me to have the pianist play and sing "There is Power in the Blood." I prayed and gave the invitation. Two of the women left, but the third one stood there holding on to the pew with a determined look on her face. A few people came to the front for prayer, then returned to their seats. The Lord spoke to me and said, "Stand steady—I'm going to save her." I appealed to the congregation to pray and told them I felt God had shown me someone was in the meeting he was going to save—though I didn't reveal that I knew who the woman was. The pianist kept singing "Power in the Blood" and we just continued to pray and wait.

"After twenty-five minutes had gone by, the woman ran to the front and fell at the altar. "I'm a Satanist," she told me. "I came here to try to put a curse on you, but it didn't work. I want to receive Jesus Christ as my Lord and renounce Satan." When I put my hand on her head to pray, she burst out speaking in tongues. The moment she confessed Christ and renounced Satan, the Holy Spirit sovereignly baptized her."

Carla said an elderly man stood up and told the people, "God used to move this way in our church, but it's been forty years since we've seen the power of God in our midst like this. We've got to get back to God."

Through the gift of discerning of spirits, Carla knew what the enemy was attempting to do in the meeting, and the Holy Spirit showed her how to pray and how to minister. She did not publicly expose the women—the Holy Spirit exposed them. The net result: one Satanist was converted, the church was revived, and Jesus was glorified.

The Holy Spirit will sharpen our discernment as we seek his guidance and remain open to his leading. One intercessor shared this: "The Lord told me, 'You are nullifying my voice when you try to talk yourself out of what I've shown you.' Most of the time, if we're obedient to God and truly walking in the Spirit, we need to go with the first impression we sense about a situation."

This same friend told us she gained a new understanding of discernment from an elderly prophet when he told her, "A person who has an agenda cannot discern."

Following is a typical example: A young single woman has been asking God for a husband. A single man, new to the congregation, begins taking her out and hints at marriage. She's so happy with the prospect, she ignores the faint stirrings of doubt. Her prayer partner warns her to be cautious. But the young woman allows her personal agenda—a desperate desire for a husband—to cancel out her ability to discern. We don't mean to imply it's wrong for a single woman to ask the Lord for a godly husband, just to warn you that your own agenda can easily distort your discernment.

Tongues.
The gift of speaking supernaturally in a language not known to the individual. The plural allows different forms, possibly harmonizing the known spoken languages of Acts 2:4-6 and the unknown transrational [i.e. speaking from the spirit instead of the intellect] utterances in Corinthians, designed particularly for praying and singing in the Spirit, mostly for private worship (see 1 Corinthians 14:14-19).

Gordon Lindsay used this explanation to help seeking believers understand the phenomenon of speaking in tongues:

A person can no more speak his natural language and also speak with other tongues at the same time than he can speak two earthly languages at once. No one would be foolish enough to try to speak English and French at the same moment. He would put away all thought of speaking one when he began to speak the other. Why not use the same common sense in regard to speaking with other tongues?[18]

Interpretation of tongues.
The gift of rendering the transrational (but not irrational) message of the Spirit meaningful to others when exercised in public. It is not the translation of a foreign language.

Ruth Friesen, one of our intercessor friends, received the baptism of the Holy Spirit in the 1930s and has spoken in at least seven different known languages. Once during the worship, Ruth sang in tongues in her strong contralto voice. Then she sang in English what she thought was the interpretation.

In the congregation was a man who had traveled to Portland from Las Vegas to attend this full gospel gathering. Following the meeting the visitor asked to meet the Jewish lady who had sung in Hebrew. When they introduced him to Ruth she assured him she was not Jewish and did not know Hebrew as he was insisting she must. He said he had been a cantor in a Jewish synagogue for seven years, and he knew the song she'd sung earlier—in exact translation, with all the half-notes. He had come to the meeting questioning the validity of tongues. "This truly was God," he said, amazed and convinced.

"He received the Holy Spirit himself, and because he was so changed, twenty other people received within a short time," Ruth told us. "I've learned just to yield my voice to the Holy Spirit and allow him to use it as he wills."

Another time, a woman left her sick bed to attend a home meeting where Ruth was present. The woman believed she'd be healed when the group prayed for her. The leaders ministering that night (including Ruth) prayed for her, but nothing seemed to happen. She said she would wait until all the others had been prayed for, so they could pray for her again.

In preparing to pray for the woman a second time, Ruth and the leaders joined hands and quietly began to pray in the Spirit. Ruth, who was standing nearest the ill woman, began speaking what sounded like an oriental language.

"My dear, my dear—God just spoke to me through you," the woman exclaimed to Ruth. "You are speaking Mandarin! I spent many years in China with my missionary parents. The Lord was saying through you, 'Why do you fear? I have nothing but gifts of love for you. Receive my gift of healing.'"

In the midst of explaining the message she'd heard in Chinese, she hesitated, then exclaimed, "I just felt the Lord's healing touch going through my body!"

Indeed she was healed, and Ruth kept in touch with that woman for years until she died in her old age.

"There are no barriers with the Holy Spirit," Ruth insists. "When I was in meetings people would come up for prayer, and I'd often sing in tongues, then sing the interpretation in English. Once a young girl told me after hearing me pray aloud in tongues that the Lord was saying to her in perfect Spanish, 'Receive my love for you, my daughter; your heavenly Father loves you.' Another time a woman in Greece understood my prayer in her language."

When Ruth was baptized in the Holy Spirit at the age of fifteen, she saw a vision of multitudes of people wailing, weeping, and milling around.

"I saw myself standing on a rough, wooden platform holding an old-fashioned lantern which was lit, swinging it back and forth, speaking in a language I did not know. The people were attracted to the light and became quiet, seeming to listen. Their troubled expressions changed to happy faces. As one, the company of people raised their hands in worship to God, their faces glowing.

"Seven times the scene changed. I would see a group of wailing people, then when they saw me swinging the light, they began to smile with joy. Each time my language changed I saw different races of people—Oriental, African, Caucasian, Hispanic, Indian."

Over the years since that night, Ruth has visited most of the nations she saw in her vision. She has brought the light of Jesus into the lives of many by allowing the Holy Spirit to use her beautiful voice to sing her prayer language.

Gifts Given by Christ

And He Himself gave some to be apostles, some prophets, some evangelists, and some pastors and teachers, for the equipping of the saints for the work of ministry, for the edifying of the body of Christ, till we all come to the unity of the faith and of the knowledge of the Son of God, to be a perfect man, to the measure of the stature of the fullness of Christ. (Ephesians 4:11-13, NKJV)

The "He Himself gave..." phrase in this passage makes it clear that the giver of the gifts listed here is Christ. The "some" makes it clear that the gifts—given to the church—are *persons* he gives to perform their appointed ministries. And the purpose is for "equipping the saints." No one function here is more infused with the Holy Spirit than are the others. The Holy Spirit is the style, the mode, the power, and the life of each ministry.

In the listings of Romans 12 and 1 Corinthians 12, gifts are given to individuals. In the Ephesians 4:11 listing, individuals are given as gifts to the church. And the purpose is to build up the saints in the church and bring them into unity. Dr. Fee observes:

Paul enumerates the *nature* of some of the "gifts" themselves and their function for the building up of the body so that it might mature in its unity.... he lists some of the gifted people who are themselves gifts to the church.... He elaborates on the role of these ministries for building up the body for maturity, soundness, and unity, drawing its life-flow from its one head, Christ Jesus.[19]

It is easy to miss seeing the real function of these ministry gifts—often called the five-fold ministries. The ministering persons are not themselves to accomplish "the work of ministry" mentioned. Rather, they are to equip all the believers (saints), who in turn are the ones who should accomplish the work.

For convenience, these five kinds of ministers can be thought of as filling "offices" in the church. But we're not instructed to classify or officially appoint each leader in the congregation as being apostle, prophet, evangelist, pastor, or teacher. The identity is recognized when the function becomes evident.

Allow the Holy Spirit to Use You

Life is like a tapestry—the stages and seasons of life change, especially for a woman. Discovering our "motivational gift" frees us to be ourselves and not try to fit into the wrong mold. On the other hand, let's be open to allowing the Holy Spirit to use us in whatever way he chooses.

PRAYER

Lord, your Word tells us that David didn't die until he had served your purpose for his generation (see Acts 13:36). I pray you will enable me to identify and acknowledge the spiritual gifts you've given me, equipping me to fulfill your purposes. Remove from me any hindrances or inhibition that would prevent your purposes from being fulfilled. Thank you, Father, for these gracious gifts which allow me to minister to others in the body of Christ. Amen.

EXERCISE

1. Review the three major passages in Scripture regarding *gifts* mentioned near the beginning of this chapter. Write down questions that occur to you as you read.

2. Write down an "analysis" of your own strengths, tendencies, and preferences in regard to the motivational gifts. Then write down opportunities for ministry available to you where these gifts can be exercised and developed.

3. Read cross-reference scriptures noted in your Bible in 1 Corinthians 12:8-10 regarding the gifts of the Holy Spirit. Write down the ways you've observed any of these gifts operating in your own life.

4. Discuss with a friend or your prayer group the questions you wrote down for item #1, and your observations from #2 and #3.

SEVEN

The Unshakable Spirit-Filled Warrior

Put on the full armor of God so that you can take your stand against the devil's schemes. For our struggle is not against flesh and blood, but against the rulers, against the authorities, against the powers of this dark world and against the spiritual forces of evil in the heavenly realms.... Pray in the Spirit on all occasions with all kinds of prayers and requests.

Ephesians 6:11-12,18a

The Holy Spirit equips us to stand firm in the midst of battles raging around us. And he teaches us how to pray.

We have an enemy named Satan. Actually, he is God's enemy, but if we are God's children, he is ours too. In the above verses the apostle Paul warns us about the enemy and his schemes or "wiles" (KJV).

The devil and his invisible demonic forces devise plans or schemes to use against us—particularly if we seem to be a threat to his kingdom of darkness. Notes in the *Companion Bible* point out that the use of the word "wiles" (in Greek, *methodeia*) in association with Satan "shows that the method or scheme is that of the devil himself, and not merely error."[1]

But God has given us his weapons: his name, his authority, the blood of Jesus, the written Word of God, praise, prayer, and the Holy Spirit's guidance.

At specific times the devil may unleash his cruelest strategies against us, striking when and where we are most vulnerable. This may happen just after we've won a spiritual victory and least expect it, or when we're so fragile from illness, weariness, or discouragement that we've let down our guard. Seasoned spiritual warriors refer to this as "backlash" or "counter-attack."

A Spiritual War Zone

Julie, a young woman who trains intercessors, experienced this recently following the Christmas holidays. While on the West Coast visiting her sister, Julie stood in the gap as an intercessor for her sister and brother-in-law, their children, and his parents and family members.

"I felt my main reason for being there that week was to pray and enter into spiritual warfare for the salvation of these people who seem totally isolated from any positive spiritual influence," Julie shared. "Members of the extended family—several of whom are immigrants from Central Europe—are involved in various cults and new age beliefs. I was the only Christian in what really was a spiritual war zone."

A breakthrough came when her brother-in-law's father, host for the traditional family Christmas dinner, singled Julie out of the large group and asked her to pray a blessing over the meal. "Apparently he wanted to acknowledge that this was a Christian holiday, even though people from other religions were present," Julie said. "He claims to be an atheist, but he has a biblical name, so I bought him a Bible and marked key scriptures which include his name. The Lord gave me great favor with both him and his wife."

Upon returning home, however, Julie was hit with such disabling depression that she was bedridden for two days. Though her life is far from being problem-free, depression and fear normally are not issues she has had to deal with.

"At first I thought maybe this was happening because I was

tired after the trip. Then the Lord showed me it was backlash from the enemy because of the effectiveness of intercession for my sister's family. I began trying to pray against the depression and fear, but it was so entrenched I just couldn't seem to pull out of it."

Although Julie is an experienced prayer warrior, this attack took her by surprise at first. But God was faithful to prompt another intercessor to pray for her and to encourage her.

"About 6:30 on a Friday morning, after I'd been awake most of the night crying and depressed, my phone rang," Julie reported. "It was a friend and intercessor I hadn't had contact with for a long time. She'd been praying for me, and the Holy Spirit had told her I was awake and that she should call. She said, 'The Lord wants you to know that he loves you, Julie, and he is pleased with you. You're being too hard on yourself!' Then she prayed part of this Psalm over me:

My help comes from the LORD, the Maker of heaven and earth. He will not let your foot slip—he who watches over you will not slumber; indeed, he who watches over Israel will neither slumber nor sleep. The LORD watches over you— the LORD is your shade at your right hand...." (Psalm 121:2-5)

It was like a phone call from heaven! Feeling overwhelmed with a sense of God's love and presence, Julie got out of bed and began praising and worshipping the Lord. The depression began to lift, and within a few hours was gone.

"When I realized that the intensity of Satan's attack against me simply revealed the power of warfare against the kingdom of darkness, I determined I would keep standing for the salvation of this family," Julie told Ruthanne. "It also reminded me of a principle I was overlooking in the midst of the experience: Praise is the most effective weapon to use against an attack of depression and fear."

Be Alert, Watchful in Prayer

A major key to heading off such attacks is remaining vigilant in prayer, and asking the Holy Spirit to keep you sensitive to his warnings. Also, it's a good idea to ask a prayer partner to cover you with intercession when you know you're going to be in a spiritual war zone. Remaining watchful in prayer doesn't come easily for most of us. But the Bible tells us:

- Be self-controlled and alert. Your enemy the devil prowls around like a roaring lion looking for someone to devour. Resist him.... (1 Peter 5:8-9a).

- Be always on the watch and pray.... (Luke 21:36a).

- ... be alert and always keep on praying.... (Ephesians 6:18b).

- Devote yourselves to prayer, being watchful and thankful (Colossians 4:2).

- ... keep watch... Watch and pray.... (Mark 14:34,38).

In conventional warfare, vigilance is essential to a successful offense against the enemy; the same is true for spiritual warfare. Arthur Mathews makes this point quite clearly:

> In warfare there are four possible attitudes—offense, defense, detente, and desertion. It is the first one of these attitudes that our adversary fears, for "Satan trembles when he sees the weakest saint upon his knees."
>
> ... The generation of Joshua's day was committed by God's command to a war of offensive action. But after Joshua arose another generation which slackened their bowstrings and sought the civilian life of coexistence by compromise. Like others, they probably argued that war is immoral and refused to see that they were blurring the distinctions between the rights of their cause as a nation under God and the evils God was using them to exterminate.
>
> ... And because of their slackened bowstrings, Satan had his heyday.

... Paul's battle language says, "Our wrestling is...." He does not say that it was or will be, but that it is a continuously present factor in our lives as Christians. And from this struggle there is no demobilization or discharge, at least in this life.[2]

God Can Make a Way

In 1993 my husband and I (Ruthanne) flew to Beijing, China, where we were to obtain visas to enter Mongolia. We had been invited to teach in the first Bible school to be established there, and were told we had pre-approved visas waiting for us at the Mongolian Embassy. I naively believed this would be a simple process.

The morning after arriving in Beijing I awakened with a headache, but also with a song ringing in my spirit—"God will make a way where there seems to be no way." Only later would I realize how meaningful this song was for that day.

Our taxi driver finally found the address we'd given him, but we were dismayed to find a huge crowd of people waiting outside the gates of the Embassy. The guards allowed only selected people to enter the gate, and when we tried to go through we were sent to the end of a very long, unruly line. Our explanations were useless, as the guards spoke no English.

The office issuing visas was open only until 11:30—which was now less than two hours away. There was no way all these people could be processed in such a short time.

A sense of hopelessness gripped me, and my head was throbbing again. "Lord, this is an impossible situation unless you help us," I prayed. "Forgive me for not being more vigilant in prayer—I should have been better prepared for this warfare. Please wake up intercessors at home and get someone praying for us."

Then suddenly I remembered the song I'd awakened with hours before, and began singing it softly. "John, we've got to believe that God is going to make a way for us," I told my husband. We began doing spiritual warfare, binding the hindering, God-hating spirits trying to block us. Then we spent the next ninety minutes standing outside that embassy praying in the Spirit or singing, "God will make a way ...."

We made it through the gate just before closing time, but as we approached the consular office they closed the door in our faces. "Tomorrow, come to the head of the line," the Mongolian official said as he locked the door. Now another problem loomed. *How can we possibly come into the city, get our visas, and still make it to the distant airport for our 9:00 a.m. flight to Mongolia?* we wondered. It looked impossible, but I kept singing my song.

Before leaving the hotel that morning we'd left our tickets with a clerk to reconfirm the next day's flight. When we returned to pick them up she told us we were confirmed, but the flight time had been changed to the afternoon. What provision!

We kept praying against any further hindrance of our mission the next morning. We were able to get our visas before noon, leaving just enough time to collect our baggage at the hotel and make it to the airport through horrendous traffic. We just kept singing, "God will make a way where there seems to be no way!" And he did just that.

Since then I try never to take anything for granted, but ask the Holy Spirit to guide me if spiritual warfare is needed and to help me remain vigilant. I also give more attention to the songs the Holy Spirit puts in my mind in the morning, or at odd times during the day. They very often indicate something meaningful about what I need to be praying for, or how the Holy Spirit will guide me during that day's events.

Testing, Temptation, or Attack?

It was Bible teacher Dean Sherman, through his book *Spiritual Warfare for Every Christian* and through his lectures, who taught me (Quin) much about the difference between testings, temptations, and the devil's attack. I learned, during a crisis, to ask myself these questions:

Is this a test from God?

Is this a temptation?

Is this an attack of the devil?

Testing develops character, endurance, patience. *Temptation* develops hatred of evil. But an *attack of Satan* makes me learn to depend on the Lord and resist the attack with Scripture: "Submit therefore to God. Resist the devil and he will flee from you" (Jas 4:7, NAS).[3]

Is it a test from God? God will test us, just as he tested the children of Israel. But the following verses reveal that his testing always has a purpose:

Remember how the LORD your God led you all the way in the desert these forty years, to humble you and to *test* you in order *to know what was in your heart....*" (Deuteronomy 8:2a, italics ours)

These are the nations the LORD left to *test* all those Israelites who had not experienced any of the wars in Canaan (he did this only to *teach* warfare to the descendants of the Israelites who had not had previous battle experience).... They were left to test the Israelites *to see whether they would obey the LORD'S commands....* (Judges 3:1-2, 4, italics ours)

Is it a *temptation?* Remember, temptation presents the opportunity to sin, it is not sin! When Mrs. Potiphar tried to get the young Joseph into bed with her, his response was, "How then could I do such a wicked thing and sin against God?" (Gn 39:9b). He refused. God gives us this promise:

No temptation has seized you except what is common to man. And God is faithful; he will not let you be tempted beyond what you can bear. But when you are tempted, he will also provide a way out so that you can stand up under it. (1 Corinthians 10:13)

Is it an attack? If I discern I'm under attack from the devil, I've learned to use scriptures in spiritual warfare to deflect his onslaught against me or my family.

When Jesus faced the temptation of Satan in the wilderness (see Luke 4:1-14) we're told he was full of the Holy Spirit, and that he used the Word of God against the attack (see Luke 4:1, 4, 8, 12). Also, being led by the Holy Spirit, he was fasting. Arthur Mathews exhorts us to learn from Jesus' example:

> Jesus took the sword of the Spirit to be His one sure weapon, His best friend in this emergency. This sword so carefully "wrought and edged by the Holy Spirit Himself" is the utterance of God and is specially designed to resist and confound Satan and all his hosts of evil.
>
> ... Therefore it is for Him to bring to the mind of the one He has led to this particular confrontation that specific utterance which He has wrought into the blade.
>
> ... There is nothing that Jesus used to defeat Satan that is not available to us. Therefore, victory is as attainable for us as it was for Him. He was filled with the Spirit, and we are expressly commanded to "be filled with the Spirit." However, let no one think that a single experience of being filled exhausts the claim of this command on our obedience.... The condition of being filled with the Holy Spirit is something to which we are required to give constant attention.[4]

Anita Fights for Her Life

When doctors gave little hope for her survival, Anita used the Word of God to fight for her life. The first hint of a blood problem came when a medical test revealed that she was pregnant. A few months later she lost her baby because of a blood clot in the placenta.

One problem followed another until finally doctors found blood clots in her brain. They diagnosed her as having an incurable blood disease. Following emergency brain surgery she seemed to be recuperating well when she suffered a stroke, after which she was unable to speak a complete sentence. She spent two and a half weeks in intensive care.

"My speech was so confused," she reported. "If I tried to say *Yes* it would come out of my mouth *No*. My husband could determine what I meant and communicate it to the doctors for me."

Before being rushed to the hospital Anita had been memorizing a scripture passage from Hebrews. Her husband had the verses printed on a large poster so she could read it easily and put it near her bed. It became her warfare scripture:

Do not, therefore, fling away your fearless confidence, for it carries a great *and* glorious compensation of reward. For you have need of steadfast patience *and* endurance, so that you may perform *and* fully accomplish the will of God, and thus receive *and* carry away [and enjoy to the full] what is promised. For still a little while—a very little while—and the Coming One will come and He will not delay. But the just shall live by faith [that is My righteous servant shall live by his conviction respecting man's relationship to God and divine things, and holy fervor born of faith and conjoined with it]; and if he draws back *and* shrinks in fear, My soul has no delight *or* pleasure in him. (Hebrews 10:35-38, TAB)

"When a doctor asked me what I was doing when I tried to read the poster aloud, I said, 'Practicing.'

"He laughed and said, 'You *will not* get your speech back by practicing.'

"But to the surprise of many, within four days, I had 98 percent of my speech back."

Doctors put Anita on a blood thinner—the same medication that earlier had caused her brain to bleed—and told her husband she still might not make it. Then while attached to so many IVs, a blood vessel in her right hand popped, causing painful swelling in her hand. A surgeon was called in, who said he didn't think they could save her hand.

"My pastor came and began to pray and read the Word of God aloud to me," Anita continued. "He read from Isaiah and this verse (41:10) gave me such comfort: 'So do not fear, for I am with you; do not be dismayed, for I am your God. I will strengthen you and help you; I will uphold you with my righteous right hand.'"

"I knew I wouldn't lose my hand—God was upholding my right hand with his righteous one. For four days in a row they performed surgery on my hand. The doctors spoke other discouraging words—like saying I'd surely have to go through rehabilitation for my hand. Since I play the piano this was a great concern. But I didn't have to undergo rehab therapy, and I can play the piano with no problem."

After she was dismissed from the hospital she had an EEG, and she prayed in the Spirit the entire time she was undergoing the test.

"They found nothing abnormal in my brain except the original blood clot," she reported. "Two months later more tests showed that the blood clot had disappeared. Now we've adopted a baby girl, and today I'm back to walking and running up to an hour a day. Through this crisis I learned the reverential fear of the Lord. He showed me his greatness and power in an incredible way. Our church had two different days of prayer and fasting for me in the midst of the crisis. The prayers of fellow believers helped carry me through."

Dixie's Assignment

Dixie, for more than eight years a Spirit-filled mom, has been praying for her son Adam, who has suffered with AIDS. When the Holy Spirit recently convicted her about her negative attitude toward Adam, she realized she'd fallen into a subtle trap of the enemy.

"Forgive me, son," she said to him. "I've mumbled and complained about you ever since you came to live with us. While I've taken care of you and prayed for you, inside I murmured."

Dixie led her son's sexual partner to the Lord before he died, and she believes Adam someday will accept the Lord's gift of salvation too. She's done her part by forgiving him, praying for him, and providing him a safe haven.

"God is working in me to love my own son unconditionally, as well as the other victims of AIDS I'm working with as a volunteer," she told Quin. "Unconditional love is what Jesus would show these people."

Together, Dixie and her husband use the Word in spiritual warfare by declaring aloud to the enemy the scriptures the Lord gives them. Praying in agreement, they come against the devil's strongholds in Adam's mind, will, and emotions.

Watchmen on the Wall

In Bible days, watchmen guarded vineyards and fields, and also stood as sentinels on city walls to watch for approaching messengers or enemies. That image is a picture of Spirit-filled intercessors keeping watch and praying over the area to which they've been assigned:

I have posted watchmen on your walls, O Jerusalem; they will never be silent day or night. You who call on the LORD, give yourselves no rest, and give him no rest till he establishes Jerusalem and makes her the praise of the earth. (Isaiah 62:6-7)

The word *watch* in the Old Testament comes from a root meaning "to hedge about (as with thorns); to guard, protect, or attend to; to be circumspect, take heed, or look narrowly."[5]

The New Testament term *to watch* means, "to chase sleep." W. E. Vine says, "The word expresses not mere wakefulness, but the watchfulness of those who are intent upon a thing."[6]

Do you see how we can allow the Holy Spirit to alert us night or day to a specific need to pray for? Or of the need to do something to clear the heaven-ways for our prayers to be answered?

Intercession Is Many-Faceted

When we (Quin and Ruthanne) intercede we see ourselves as standing between God and a particular person, beseeching God on his or her behalf. We also see ourselves as standing between that person and Satan, doing spiritual battle. It seems accurate to say then that *intercession* is *intervention*.

How do we as busy women find time to pray? We believe each of us can carve out some minutes to be alone and talk to the Lord—committing our day to him, asking him to order our steps and our conversation, and generally "checking in" with him for the day. Our special time—whether a few minutes or a longer period—should include worship, prayer, and Bible reading/study. But think of other creative times to pray.

You can pray for your family members while you make the beds, wash the clothes, vacuum the house, prepare the meals, iron the shirts, drive the carpools. Busy career women can pray en route to work, in elevators, while waiting for appointments, or in grocery check-out lines.

Once I (Ruthanne) heard a teacher who suggested that while driving, we should practice "intersection intercession." Instead of becoming annoyed with the inattentive or careless drivers we encounter, we can pray for them—as well as others we see while waiting at intersections.

After hearing this suggestion, I began noticing the people in cars around me as I drove. One morning as I waited at a traffic light, I saw a husband and wife embroiled in an argument with the wife in tears. I began asking the Holy Spirit to release his peace into that situation and to help them work out their problems.

Another time I was stopped at the scene of an accident where policemen were trying to get a driver out of his damaged car that had been hit broadside. I asked the Lord to give them wisdom for how to release the man and prayed that the trauma of the experience would cause him to call upon the Lord.

In my city we often see homeless people standing at intersections with signs asking for help. As the Holy Spirit leads, I sometimes give them money or food, but mostly I try always to pray for the homeless people I come upon as I drive around the city.

Closet of Your Heart

My friend Joan Morton, president of Aglow International for Australia, introduced me (Quin) to the concept of "the secret closet of my heart" as a place of prayer. Paramount to this idea is allowing the Holy Spirit to pray through her. Joan says:

The Holy Spirit is a creative facilitator of the will and the heart of God. Because He is also the One who indwells us, who brings out the cry of our own hearts and melds it with the heart of God, somehow He reaches out of our spirit into the heavenlies where God dwells. Then whatever is in us—crying or groaning or weeping—is a prayer to the Father prayed from the closet of the heart.[7]

When Joan read in Exodus 28 about the holy garments God instructed the Israelites to make for members of the priesthood, she realized it was a significant message for her too. The high priest was to wear a breastplate containing twelve precious stones, each stone representing one of the tribes with its name inscribed on it. When he went before the Lord, he was bearing the names and concerns of Israel's twelve clans or families over his heart, and in essence, presenting them to the Lord:

Whenever Aaron enters the Holy Place, he will bear the names of the sons of Israel over his heart on the breastpiece of decision as a continuing memorial before the LORD. (Exodus 28:29)

Other translations say "before the Lord *continually*."

Joan realized that in the New Testament Paul called believers "priests." Thus, because as a believer she is a priest, she could bring names continually before the Lord in her heart. Joan continues:

As the Holy Spirit opened this truth to me, I saw that as I let God know my spirit was open to Him to speak to me, He could give me names of more people that I could wear daily on my breastplate and have on my heart all day and even all night, people who were involved in many, many situations and circumstances.

I found as I put on, as it were, my breastplate, the Holy Spirit would daily quicken to me names to be inscribed on the stones. Some were placed there for a length of time, but as I knew in my spirit that the Holy Spirit had prayed through these names, He would give me another name, and other circumstances to pray for.

... As I went to work, to ministry, or to the market, I knew that those names were on the breastplate and in my spirit; they were continually before the Lord. What a precious place the closet of the heart is. What a sacred place it is.[8]

Prayer: A Continual Way of Living

Joan began to teach Christian women throughout Australia not to feel condemned if they couldn't spend several hours in prayer a day, because even busy women can find time to pray— without struggling or striving. "God wants our praying to become a continual way of living," she told Quin. "We can expect the Holy Spirit to come to us with thoughts and impressions and we will be quickened to pray right then in the closet of our hearts."

Even one of our "biblical grandmothers" gave us this example. "Hannah was praying in her heart, and her lips were moving but her voice was not heard..." (1 Sm 1:13a). Many of us can identify with this type of praying.

I (Quin) encourage women to pray every day for their specific assignments from God before they begin their daily routine. This includes prayer for your immediate family, extended family, special friends, church staff, city, country, and other nations of the world that the Lord lays on your heart.[9]

One of the ways I have seen the Holy Spirit's faithful direction has been through the prayer journals I've kept for more than twenty years. In them I have recorded my prayers, scripture verses I felt the Lord gave me in prayer, and later how and when he answered. Some of the prayers recorded in those journals are yet to be answered—but I haven't stopped praying. LeRoy and I have cried out to God in prayer—and in our journals—for him to give us direction, help us sell our houses, provide the right jobs for our children, show us where to move, and send the right people into our lives. As I re-read my journals from time to time, I can clearly see how the Holy Spirit led us at times when we were not even aware of it.

Most of all I've learned I must persevere in prayer!

A Warrior Is Persistent

We see an example of persistence in the prophet Elijah, who prophesied to wicked King Ahab that it would rain and end the three-year drought which he himself had brought about through prayer (see 1 Kings 18). Though he had God's assurance, Elijah still prayed seven times before even a cloud the size of a man's hand appeared in the sky and rain finally fell. We don't know how much time passed between his first and seventh prayer, as he crouched down on the ground with his face between his knees beseeching God. This was a typical birthing position for women of that time. Elijah was birthing his prayer in persistence.

Or you might say, as Bible teacher Dutch Sheets explains, *"He was releasing the power of God into the situation."*

God wants our participation in what he desires to bring about in the earth. Even the New Testament talks about Elijah:

> The earnest (heart-felt, continued) prayer of a righteous man makes tremendous power available—dynamic in its working. Elijah was a human being with a nature such as we have—with feelings, affections and constitution as ourselves; and he prayed earnestly for it not to rain, and no rain fell on the earth for three years and six months. (James 5:16b-17, TAB)

Daniel prayed twenty-one days before God's messenger broke through in spiritual warfare to come in answer to his prayer. The angel said:

> Since the first day that you set your mind to gain understanding and to humble yourself before your God, your words were heard, and I have come in response to them. But the prince of the Persian kingdom resisted me twenty-one days. Then Michael, one of the chief princes, came to help me, because I was detained there with the king of Persia. (Daniel 10:12-13)

This was war in the heavenlies. What if Daniel had quit on the tenth day? Or on the twentieth day? No, he persisted. And God's angel got through with a word for Daniel in answer to his prayer.

Overcoming Our Hesitancy

Jesus himself tells a parable illustrating tenacious prayer (see Luke 11). A friend goes at midnight to his neighbor's door, persistently knocking as he asks for three loaves of bread for his unexpected guests. He knocks and knocks until he gets what he came for. Notice how specific he was: three loaves was his goal.

This parable is not about annoying God until we get what we want. Nor is it about overcoming God's reluctance. It's about overcoming our own hesitancy to ask with shameless boldness.

> I tell you, although he will not get up and supply him anything because he is his friend, yet because of his shameless persistence *and* insistence, he will get up and give him as much as he needs. So I say to you, Ask *and* keep on asking, and it shall be given you; seek *and* keep on seeking, and you shall find; knock *and* keep on knocking, and the door shall be opened to you. For everyone who asks *and* keeps on asking receives, and he who seeks *and* keeps on seeking finds, and to him who knocks *and* keeps on knocking the door shall be opened. (Luke 11:8-10, TAB)

I (Quin) have this note scribbled in my Bible, based on the study notes in *The Spirit-filled Life Bible* commentary on Luke 11:

1. The Father is more than my friend. He's on my side, available anytime.
2. Boldness is my privilege. I will come with shameless persistence to pray as the Holy Spirit directs. Ask. Seek. Knock.

> Jesus teaches persistence in prayer, along with a sense of urgency and boldness.... The three imperatives are in the Greek present tense, denoting a continuous asking, seeking, and knocking.... The praying is ours to do; unless we ask for the intervention of his kingdom and obey his prayer-lessons, nothing will change. All kingdom ministry begins with, is sustained by, and will triumph through prayer.[10]

We encourage you to become persistent in your praying. You may want to pray the following prayer for those whom you're trusting God to bring to salvation. Be open to the Holy Spirit's leading to add other ideas as you pray. Your prayer is not rote repetition, nor a mechanical exercise. The flow of the Holy Spirit will keep your praying fresh.

PRAYER

Heavenly Father, I come to you on behalf of ___(name)___ , and I thank you for the assurance of your Word that you are not willing for him to perish. I pray that he be delivered from spiritual blindness, and from every scheme and snare the devil has used to hold him captive. Let every stronghold of unbelief and vain imagination in his life be pulled down and brought into captivity to the obedience of Christ.

Father, please speak to him by the Holy Spirit, revealing to him that he must call upon you to be saved—and give him the desire to do it. Lord of the harvest, send laborers across his path to share the gospel and speak into his life, and prepare his heart to receive their words. I thank you that ___(name)___ 's life will fulfill the purpose for which you created him, and that he will honor and glorify you. I pray this in Jesus' name, Amen.

EXERCISE

1. *Identify* the areas where the enemy most often attacks you: fear, anxiety, worry, grief, guilt, addictions, occult or cult involvement, unforgiveness, rejection. God's enemy seeks to make women feel inferior, unworthy, unloved. Don't allow it; ask the Holy Spirit for a battle plan to overcome in your vulnerable areas (see our book *A Woman's Guide to Breaking Bondages* published by Servant Publications).

2. Identify the prayer assignment God has given you—your family, unsaved relatives, your church, your city, and certain nations he has put on your heart to pray for.

3. Start a prayer diary to record the words the Holy Spirit speaks to you during prayer. Record scriptures he quickens you to pray over those he's called you to pray for.

4. Put up a "prayer board" poster or bulletin board with pictures of those you are praying for and a small map of the countries you most often pray about.

5. Following are a few scriptures to help you get started in praying the Word of God for your unsaved loved ones:

   Matthew 18:12-14

   2 Timothy 2:25b, 26

   Acts 26:18

   2 Corinthians 4:3-6

   2 Corinthians 10:4-5

   2 Peter 3:8-9

6. Read some of the above scriptures in various translations. For example, 2 Corinthians 10:3-5 in The Living Bible states:

   > It is true that I am an ordinary, weak human being, but I don't use human plans and methods to win my battles. I use God's mighty weapons, not those made by men, to knock down the devil's strongholds. These weapons can break down every proud argument against God and every wall that can be built to keep men from finding him. With these weapons I can capture rebels and bring them back to God, and change them into men whose hearts' desire is obedience to Christ.

7. Do a word study on some of the key passages and apply them to your prayer life. For example, study the word *stronghold:* a fortified place like a castle that seems impenetrable. A stronghold can be a thought pattern, or ideas that control or govern a person's thinking. It can be a mind-set of hopelessness that causes a person to accept a situation as being unchangeable—even something we know is contrary to the will of God. We can use the Word of God to destroy these strongholds.

❧

EIGHT

Praying in the Spirit

For if I pray in a tongue, my spirit prays, but my mind is unfruitful. So what shall I do? I will pray with my spirit, but I will also pray with my mind....

1 Corinthians 14:14-15a

...pray in the Spirit on all occasions with all kinds of prayers and requests.

Ephesians 6:18a

To "pray with the spirit" involves both your human spirit and the Holy Spirit. Receiving Christ as Savior not only reconciles you to God, it also enables you to communicate directly with God "through the power of the Holy Spirit."[1] This mystical reality—which bypasses human logic—must be received by your human spirit, not your mind.

Pastor Chuck Pierce, a gifted leader of intercessors and one of our colleagues in the Spiritual Warfare Network, says: "Praying in the Spirit—or praying in tongues—brings the believer's mind into alignment with the Holy Spirit, opening the mind and clearing the way to hear from God. It also breaks through demonic forces that are working in a person's life, or trying to hinder or confuse what the Spirit of God is saying. This allows the mind to aid the human spirit in comprehending the will and purpose of God—which is the basic truth of Romans 8:26-27."

Driven to God and Prayer

Barbara is a woman like many we've met whose desperate circumstances drove her to God and to prayer. When she married Eldon as a teenager she didn't know he was addicted to drugs. Five years and two children later, frustrated with feeling her husband would never change, Barbara got a divorce. She committed her life to Christ, began attending church, and sought God's help for the problems she faced as a single parent.

"Although I wasn't brought up in church, I knew my mother was a woman of prayer," Barbara reported. "I relied on her prayers for my life. I had gone to various prayer meetings, but always felt inadequate because I didn't know what to say to God. But one day I heard a minister describe my life exactly: a person who has an assurance of salvation, believes the Word of God, goes to church, but has no victory in everyday life. He invited those who felt that way to come forward for prayer to receive the Holy Spirit—so they could begin walking in victory."

Barbara went forward. The minister laid hands on her, asking the Lord to baptize her with the Holy Spirit.

"I knew by faith that I'd received God's gift, although I didn't speak with tongues as many of those around me did," she said. "But later, I knelt in my bedroom to pray and told the Lord I wasn't getting up until I was able to speak in tongues. I knew nothing about the Holy Spirit, but neither did I have any prejudice against tongues. Somehow the Lord helped me to yield to him that night, and I prayed in tongues, then began searching Scripture to learn more about the Holy Spirit."

An Urgency to Intercede

With no help from Eldon, Barbara's job provided the sole support for her children's needs. But six years after her divorce, her job was cut in a series of company layoffs. Though she had more time to pray, she had no visible means of support. Then late one night she had an unusual experience.

"About 2:00 A.M. the Holy Spirit awakened me," she reported. "As I lay in bed meditating on the Word of God, the phone rang. It was Eldon, my ex-husband. He had heard that I'd been laid off from my job around Christmas time and was calling to express concern. 'I love my children,' he said."

"You don't know what love is," Barbara replied sharply. "The Bible says that because God loved, he *gave* his son. Loving means giving. Until you understand that truth, don't ever tell us again that you love us. You never give anything to support your children, nor are you now prepared to—and you rarely visit them."

Enraged by her words, Eldon began cursing her on the telephone. She responded by praying in tongues. The cursing stopped and he said, "I know what that is—I've heard that kind of talking before." Abruptly, he hung up.

After the call Barbara left her bed with an urgency to continue praying. She felt the Holy Spirit revealed that Eldon was facing imminent destruction unless intercession was made.

"I knew his deliverance could only come from God, so I just gave myself to the Lord in intercession," she said. "I prayed in tongues for what seemed like a long period of time, as the Holy Spirit took full control of my prayer. Later, as the burden began to lift and I sensed a breakthrough, warm tears of joy began flowing down my cheeks. I heard the Spirit of God whisper in my spirit, 'He is delivered.'"

Three days later Eldon called again. "I don't know what you were saying when you were speaking that language on the phone the other night," he said. "But something happened." He claimed he hadn't taken any drugs since then. He wanted to know more about pursuing a relationship with God. In meetings he'd attended with a friend he had heard people speak in tongues, and he knew it was a valid experience.

Barbara shared how she had received the Holy Spirit and also explained to him the plan of salvation. Eldon told her he had repented and accepted Christ during the three days since his phone call, and asked if he could go to church with Barbara and the children. He began attending regularly, and soon gave his testimony before the congregation.

"Eldon never went back to drugs after that experience, and five months later we were remarried," Barbara told us. "Some may have felt I needed to wait a longer time for him to prove himself, but I did what I felt God led me to do. The children were thrilled to have a father—the younger one actually had few memories of his daddy because he had been a baby at the time of the divorce. We've been remarried for fourteen years now. It's the most miraculous deliverance I have ever seen by the power of the Holy Spirit and through praying in tongues."

Today, with Eldon's encouragement and support, Barbara devotes her life to teaching and training intercessors—both in the U.S. and abroad. "I was born to intercede," she says.

Praying Beyond Our Knowledge

Bible commentator Arthur Wallis says:

...the Holy Spirit is able to illuminate our minds when we are praying over some matter with inadequate knowledge. But there are times when we do not need to know the facts—perhaps important that we do *not* know. It is here that praying with the Spirit may take over from praying with the mind, enabling us to pray beyond our knowledge of the situation, because the Holy Spirit who inspires the language knows all the facts.... Although we do not know what we are saying, it is enough to know that the Holy Spirit is inspiring it, and that the prayer will therefore be right "on target." What does it matter that we do not understand the words when we know that God does?[2]

Bypassing Selfish Desires

Praying is a spiritual activity, yet a person may be motivated by unspiritual desires to pray for the wrong thing, with tragic results. We heard from a woman detailing the misery and heartache she was having with her new husband. She says she had prayed specifically, "God, I want a godly husband, and I want __(name)__." The problem was, she was already living with him. She knew he was not a godly man, she had already seen his character flaws, and her friends had warned her against marrying him. Yet she went on with the wedding, and now wanted God to deliver her from the suffering she was enduring due to her willfulness.

A young professional woman we know, on the other hand, learned the difference between depending on the Holy Spirit and listening to her own emotions or feelings—often called the "soul realm." She was offered a fine home, furs, jewelry, and a well-behaved stepson if she would just marry her boss. Because he wasn't a Christian, she first led him to the Lord. But as she prayed about marrying him, the Holy Spirit put a check in her spirit. "Just wait... God has something better." She chose to turn down material possessions to wait for a righteous man of God's choosing. And she is still waiting, with no regrets.

Soulish prayer says, "I want what I want when I want it." Spirit-led prayer says, "Whatever you want, Lord. Give me the grace to accept it and walk in it without complaining."

Many of us allow the soulish area of our lives—mind, will, emotions—to control even our prayer life. But instead of telling the Lord what is best for us, we need to practice asking the Holy Spirit to guide our prayers.

Overcoming Your Reluctance

It's true that this matter of speaking in tongues has become for some Christians a bone of doctrinal contention. The practice seems so bizarre and illogical to some that they find it hard to accept, even when they find it taught in the Bible. In many cases God has allowed special circumstances in individuals' lives to bring them to a place of acceptance.

Fran and Mike are long-time friends of mine (Quin's) who

were led to the Lord by the Dutch evangelist Corrie ten Boom. They became close friends, and Corrie and her traveling companion spent many restful holidays in Fran and Mike's home in Florida.

Eight years after my friends had met Jesus, they visited Corrie at a Christian camp where she was speaking. One afternoon as Corrie and Fran were taking a walk, Corrie asked, "Frances, would you like me to pray for Jesus to baptize you in the Holy Spirit?"

"Yes, I would," Fran replied.

They stopped on the path, then Corrie laid hands on her and prayed for the Lord Jesus to baptize her with the Holy Spirit. "Fran, now you can pray in tongues if you wish," Corrie said.

Fran studied her friend's beautiful wrinkled face, then shaking her head replied, "I don't wish to." They finished their walk, returned to the camp dormitory, and Corrie never mentioned the matter of tongues to Fran again.

"The idea of speaking in tongues scared me," Fran later told me. "I was afraid of losing control of my own tongue after a lifetime of being taught to be careful what I say. The idea of someone else speaking through me was frightening. Also, I didn't have a scriptural understanding of tongues. But Corrie never pressured me. Because I didn't 'feel' anything when she prayed, nor immediately thereafter see any significant change in my life, I wasn't really sure whether I had been baptized in the Holy Spirit or not."

A Divine Appointment

A short while later Fran and Mike were visiting the same church in Destin, Florida, where I had received the Holy Spirit some years earlier. As the pastor finished his message he invited all those who had not been baptized in the Holy Spirit to go to a room at the back of the sanctuary. There his wife would instruct them and pray for them.

Fran and Mike rather reluctantly went to the back room with the group of seekers. But when the pastor's wife mentioned that the gift of tongues is available for believers today, Fran once again hesitated to have prayer for this gift. Following her experience with Corrie at the Christian camp, she had met an evangelist named Chris and heard him speak about tongues. His teaching sounded solid, and she respected him. So she prayed, "Lord, if you want me to speak in tongues, I'll just wait, and if Chris ever comes back to Florida again, I'll have him pray for me."

She had barely breathed that prayer when she looked up to see Chris walk through the door into the room! He had been driving through Destin, headed for another town, when the Holy Spirit told him to stop and go into St. Andrew church. He sat down with the congregation, expecting to hear something in the pastor's message to clarify why the Lord had directed him to make this stop. But he immediately felt led to get up and go down the hall to the last door on the right.

"Fran, Dr. Mike, what are you doing here?" he asked when he saw them. They were among the few in the room he recognized.

"I guess I was waiting for you," Fran stammered, barely able to speak. "Will you pray for me to receive my prayer language?" He was delighted at the request. When Chris prayed for her, Fran spoke only a few halting words, but he encouraged her to allow the Holy Spirit to continue speaking these words through her during her prayer time. Then he left to continue his journey.

Praying the Will of the Father

Over the next two months Fran became more fluent as she prayed in tongues two or three hours a day. But during her prayer time she noticed that the same few syllables were often repeated.

One morning after prayer she turned on the TV just as a talk show host was saying, "We are honored today to have the new president of Egypt with us. Welcome Mr. Anwar Sadat." Fran moved closer to the TV and listened intently as the host again pronounced the Egyptian president's name. She suddenly realized that was the name she had been saying for the past several weeks while praying in tongues.

"I could feel the hair rise up on my neck," she reported. "I realized God had been directing my prayer as I used my prayer language, and that this man was important to God. I saw that, by way of tongues, the Holy Spirit can pray through yielded believers, thus influencing current world leaders and events those individuals may know nothing about. We have the potential to pray the perfect will of the Father by allowing the Holy Spirit to pray through us."

Fran later prayed for a young woman brought to her home after she had hit a wall while riding a horse. After Fran prayed for her—some of the time in tongues—the young woman, who was studying Spanish in college, said, "You are quoting healing scriptures in Castilian Spanish. You are saying that by Jesus' stripes, I am healed." She was shocked to know that a prayer language could be a language that she herself understood but that Fran, who was praying, did not know. Because of these experiences, Fran now almost daily prays in tongues for long periods of time as she intercedes for others.

Diversity in Prayer

...Pray in the Spirit on all occasions with all kinds of prayers and requests. With this in mind, be alert and always keep on praying for all the saints. (Ephesians 6:18)

In the above verse Paul urges believers to "pray in the Spirit," but the passage also suggests diversity—"all kinds of prayers and requests." In 1 Corinthians 14:14-15, Paul encouraged believers to pray in tongues, and also to pray with their understanding.

Barbara's and Fran's testimonies are examples of how praying in tongues led to dramatic results. But to "pray in the Spirit" also can mean to be specifically led by the Holy Spirit as to how to pray "with your mind" in your own language for a given circumstance.

I (Ruthanne) remember a time ten years ago when my husband and I were on a ministry trip to southern France and I became ill. Cindy, my prayer partner back in Texas, not knowing any details, felt the Holy Spirit prompting her to pray that the Lord would strengthen my immune system. That was the focus of her prayer for me for several days. I managed to complete the itinerary, but was checked by a doctor when I got home and treated for a kidney infection. Though total healing didn't come through prayer, I know Cindy's prayers helped me to get home on schedule and safely so the problem could be treated.

Being Available to God

Very likely you've had the experience of suddenly having a person's name come to mind, or of having a dream about an individual. We suggest you treat such an occurrence as a call from the Holy Spirit to pray for that person or situation. Often as you begin to pray about things you already know about, the Holy Spirit will reveal additional things which need prayer coverage. Other times you may do as Barbara did, and just pray in tongues until the burden lifts.

Johannes Facius, who directs an international prayer ministry in Europe, reminds us of the nature of true prayer:

Prayer is not our bringing before the Lord all the things that we think are important; but prayer is our coming to the point where we are available to listen to what the Lord wants us to deal with in prayer, whatever that might be. If we cannot learn to empty ourselves before God and unwind our busy minds and put down every anxious thought we might have, we will never come to the place where we will be able to allow the Holy Spirit to begin to inspire us and help us in prayer.

The total success of intercessory prayer depends on the source of our intercession—whether the things we are interceding for have been appointed by God, or whether they are of our own choice, our own emotions, or our own burdens. If they come from ourselves and we try to get the Lord to go along with them, it is in fact we who are choosing Him for that which we feel is important. But when we are in that to which He appoints us, we will see fruit of our labour; we will receive answers to our prayers, and the outcome of our intercessory ministry will be fruit for eternity; fruit that will remain.[3]

Many women of prayer have told us of times when the Holy Spirit alerted them to pray for someone they didn't know—sometimes a person they had seen only in passing, sometimes a total stranger, sometimes a public figure or celebrity. It may be a long-term prayer assignment from the Holy Spirit, or it may be a one-time call to prayer for the moment. Kerry, one of Quin's prayer partners, shared with us her own such experience.

"Once I awoke in the middle of the night and prayed in tongues for what seemed like a long time. I only knew my prayer language was being used to war in the heavenlies for something I didn't understand.

"After the prayer stopped I asked the Lord, 'What was that all about?' He showed me the face of a man I scarcely knew, except that I'd seen him leading the singing in a Sunday school class. 'Why me, Lord?' I asked again. I felt the Lord's answer was sufficient when he impressed this thought on my heart: 'Because he is in danger, and you are the only person who is willing to wake right now and do warfare on his behalf.' We don't always know the outcome of such prayers, but I have since been willing to pray night or day for anyone God impresses upon me by the Spirit."

Hearing God for Your Circumstances

I (Quin) had an experience many mothers can relate to. While my daughter Sherry was attending college in a nearby city, I grew concerned when she didn't come home Easter weekend or call to let us know her plans. Since this was unusual for her, I called, but her roommate said she wasn't there. As I prayed, the Holy Spirit showed me exactly where she had gone.

I drove to that place, knocked on the door and asked for her as if I were expecting her to be there. When she came down the stairs and found me waiting, she apologized for not coming home or calling us. She was grieved because we'd learned her grandmother had a short time to live and she had been very close to her. Not knowing if she could deal with her emotions upon seeing her grandmother if she came home, she had chosen to go home with a friend to escape. But she did go home with me and we all enjoyed being with Mom for her last Easter.

Many Christian moms have this Holy Spirit-guided "radar" that alerts them when their children are in trouble. The Holy Spirit may reveal where they are, or unfold God's plan for how to reach them during their season of unrest.

As one mom prayed about a withdrawn teenager who didn't think she was loved as much as her siblings, she asked the Lord for a way to show love to this child. The Holy Spirit's inspired idea was so practical it seemed almost too easy: "Rearrange your schedule to spend more time with her, from taking her along for grocery shopping to letting her cook supper with you. Take her to school basketball games. Just spend time with her doing what's important to her."

It worked. Not overnight, but gradually her daughter responded. It was the Holy Spirit's way of reaching one child during a difficult period of her life.

Groans Too Deep for Words

Then there is a way of "praying in the Spirit" which employs what Scriptures calls *groans*:

> In the same way, the Spirit helps us in our weakness. We do not know what we ought to pray, but the Spirit himself intercedes for us with groans that words cannot express. And he who searches our hearts knows the mind of the Spirit, because the Spirit intercedes for the saints in accordance with God's will. (Romans 8:26-27)

Various scholars interpret this passage to mean different things. Some say it refers to silent prayer; others believe it means inarticulate groans motivated by the Holy Spirit; still others believe, particularly in light of Paul's statements in 1 Corinthians 14, that it means praying in tongues. Dr. Fee writes:

> Origen [a third-century church father] probably had it right, in understanding these sentences as a whole and this phrase in particular [v. 26b] to refer to a kind of private ("to oneself") praying in tongues that Paul speaks about as part of his resolution of the practice of uninterpreted tongues in the worshiping community in Corinth.
>
> ... Rather than seeing praying in the Spirit ("tongues speech" if you will) as some sort of mindless activity, Paul sees it as a highly significant expression of prayer. In it the believer can take special encouragement even in the midst of present... weaknesses... for the Spirit is praying in keeping with God's will and with "inarticulate groanings" that God himself well understands, since he knows the mind of the Spirit. One may not understand how all of that works out in practice, but Paul, at least, sees it as a powerful encouragement from the "firstfruits" of the Spirit.[4]

One intercessor, who is childless, says the Holy Spirit often directs her to pray concerning the plight of abused and rejected children in our society. "As I identify with their horrendous suffering and the pain of their rejection, I find myself weeping, groaning, and travailing in prayer," she said. "I may never know in this life the result of my intercession, but I know that, according to Romans 8:27, I'm praying God's will in the situation. Such travail truly can be painful, but there's great satisfaction in knowing you've obeyed the Holy Spirit and touched God's heart."

Praying in a Language Others Understand

Jennie is an excellent example of an intercessor allowing the Holy Spirit to pray through her. Some Christian friends living near her who were former Moslems often asked her to pray for the salvation of their relatives still living in the Middle East. Jennie took the prayer assignment seriously, and she often found herself interceding for them during the night hours.

When she heard that the mother and brother of her friend, Sam, were coming to the United States for a two-week visit, Jennie invited them all to her home for a meal.

As they visited that evening, Jennie led the mother to the Lord. Not only did she receive Jesus, she was baptized in the Holy Spirit and began to speak in other tongues.

Jennie then asked Sam's thirty-year-old brother—with Sam translating into Arabic—if he wanted to accept Jesus as his mother had just done.

"I have no religion. I have no religion," he said emphatically, shaking his head.

"It's not a religion, but a relationship with Jesus," Jennie explained.

"No religion. I have no religion," he repeated.

"Do you mind if I pray for God to reveal himself to you?" Jennie asked.

"OK," he replied, "OK."

The rest of the group knelt with Jennie at the young man's feet and began to pray in tongues. When everyone else quit, Jennie kept praying. "I was so mad at the devil for keeping this man in bondage, I kept praying in tongues until I finally felt a release," she said.

Sam's wife shouted, "Jennie, you have been binding the devil in the Arabic language!"

The young man's eyes got big as he stared at Jennie. He knew she didn't know his native language, but he had recognized the words Jennie used. "The headache I've had all evening long just left!" he told her, with Sam interpreting.

"Are you ready now to accept Jesus as Lord and Savior?" Jennie asked again.

"Yes, yes!" he shouted.

With great joy she led him in a prayer of repentance. "The work of the Holy Spirit to allow this man to hear me praying in his own language was the key to his salvation," Jennie told Quin. "What a thrill to see this result after months of intercession."

Praying for Others to Receive

When we meet the Holy Spirit in a new way, we yearn for others to know him as we do. Sometimes we risk being offensive, trying to force a book or a meeting on our husbands, our children, or our friends. But we're not called to try to *be* the Holy Spirit in their lives. Instead, we can simply pray that God will reveal himself to them in his own way.

Jo's life was radically changed when she received the Holy Spirit and spoke in tongues. She began praying that her husband, Ron, who was a nominal Christian, would have the same experience. She remained active in their denominational church, but also attended a weekly Bible study held at an independent church.

"At least Ron would listen as I shared spiritual insights I was learning at the Bible study," she said. "One day he told me, 'Jo,

I may not understand all that God is doing in your life, but I am very impressed.'"

Because of Ron's quiet nature, Jo was careful not to belittle him or to push him, and she saw signs that Ron was maturing in his faith. "Lord, please let it be so natural for Ron to receive the Holy Spirit that it will be as easy as falling off a log," was her prayer.

One Sunday the Lord dropped an idea into her heart. Since they were one flesh, she could pray for Ron just as she prayed for herself. She thought of areas in Ron's life for which he may not have thought to ask forgiveness and that he had not renounced. "As the Lord brought these things to mind, I prayed, asking God's forgiveness for Ron's involvement in anything not pleasing to him, and I renounced them," she reported.

Then one night when she attended a meeting at the independent church, one of their fellow church members was baptized in the Holy Spirit and spoke in tongues. Driving home she felt sorry for herself because it seemed Ron showed no interest in receiving the Holy Spirit as these other men did.

"David received the baptism in the Holy Spirit tonight," she said with an edge to her voice when she found Ron in the garage. "Maybe it would happen to you too if you'd ever put yourself in a place where God could touch you that way."

As she got ready for bed the Holy Spirit convicted her for her judgmental attitude, and she repented before the Lord. When Ron came to bed he said, "Jo, just when I think I'm doing pretty well, you say something like you said tonight. Did you ever think that maybe I'd like the baptism of the Holy Spirit to happen to me, too?"

Jo apologized for her sarcasm and asked for Ron's forgiveness. "But God puts a holy jealousy in us to draw us into the things of God," she explained. "Would you like to receive right now?"

Ron put his hand in hers and said, "Yes, pray for me." Jo had never prayed with anyone to receive the Holy Spirit all by herself. She gulped and silently prayed for help. Then she asked aloud for the Lord to baptize Ron with the Holy Spirit. "Just begin to praise the Lord quietly," she said, not wanting him to feel awkward.

After maybe a minute, he opened his eyes. "Can I say this out loud?" he asked.

"Of course!" Jo replied.

The Lord began to cause words to float through his mind in the form of a melody—though he had never been musical. As he began singing out these words he received the baptism as easily as falling off a log, just as Jo had requested!

"Today we remain active in our denominational church," she reports. "The Lord is using Ron as an elder to bring balance and encouragement in the spiritual and administrative aspects of our church. God has been faithful."

Strengthened in the Spirit

… Build yourselves up in your most holy faith and pray in the Holy Spirit. (Jude 1:20)

He who speaks in a tongue edifies himself.… (1 Corinthians 14:4)

These verses tell us that praying in tongues is a way to build up or strengthen your own faith. In other words, praying in the Spirit is not only a means of intercession for others, but a means of receiving strength from the Holy Spirit.

Corrie ten Boom writes:

A missionary in China had to endure brainwashing. He resisted and fought against it, but the moment came when he felt he was at the end of his strength. Then he started to pray in tongues. That fellowship with the Lord, in absolute relaxation, was his salvation. The enemy could not influence his mind any longer. I believe that the Lord has given this gift at this time to many of His children in many different churches and groups, because it is a strong weapon and will prove to be so in the final battle. It is a fact that nothing has received so much criticism and opposition, even among believing Christians, as has this gift, which is described so clearly in the Word of God. Paul says in 1 Corinthians 14:5 (Phillips): "I should indeed like you all to speak in tongues." The "God is dead" theology and occultism, which are practiced even by Christians, receive less criticism and resistance, yes, and even enmity, than this gift from the Spirit....[5]

Pastor Ted Haggard says, "Times of prayer are always dominated by something—our self-pity, our sin, our family needs or need for money, or His Spirit and His kingdom. The primary way to turn away from our own interests and become absorbed by His is to pray in the Spirit.... I find that as I pray in tongues, my priorities and thoughts are sharpened. My attitudes change, my inner man is strengthened, my faith is increased, and God drops fresh ideas into my mind."[6]

Praying in tongues has another benefit. When we pray in the Holy Spirit we are building ourselves up. It is for self-edification (see 1 Corinthians 4:4). "But you, beloved, building yourselves up on your most holy faith, praying in the Holy Spirit, keep yourselves in the love of God...." (Jude 1:20-21a, NKJV)

PRAYER
Lord, help me to be conscious that when I don't know how to pray, you allow the Holy Spirit to pray through me. Help me be more alert to your still, small voice calling me to prayer. I want to be more cooperative and yielded! Thank you that this gift of praying in the Spirit also will strengthen me. I need that desperately. Again I give thanks that you loved me enough to send your Holy Spirit. Amen.

NINE

❦

Our Expectations—
God's Intervention

*"For my thoughts are not your thoughts, neither are your
ways my ways," declares the LORD.*

Isaiah 55:8

*But I tell you the truth: It is for your good that I am going
away. Unless I go away, the Counselor will not come to you;
but if I go, I will send him to you.*

John 16:7

The Holy Spirit can move through us with his power, bringing God's supernatural intervention to our various situations and crises. He also can move sovereignly, without our
participation. But he doesn't always move *when* and *how* we
may expect.

Jesus' followers were devastated enough by the thought that
he was going away. But to hear him say, "It is for your good" was
unthinkable. They saw no value in his sending someone else.
How could anything good come from seeing their Lord unjustly
crucified at the hands of evil men? The plan was too big for
their small vision to embrace.

Only after the cross did they understand the truth of his mes-
sages to them. Only after Pentecost, as the Holy Spirit moved
through them in power, could they appreciate his gift, the
Counselor.

His plans and purposes for his people far exceed anything

we can imagine with our limited understanding. It was true when Isaiah wrote his revelation: "For my thoughts are not your thoughts, neither are your ways my ways, declares the LORD." And it's still true today. He can be as gentle as a breeze or as mighty as a hurricane, but he does not perform to suit our expectations or demands. Nor will he be limited by our weak faith or human reasoning.

All of us—whether baby Christians or mature ones—face times when we think we can't make it through our difficulties. That's when we need to experience the Holy Spirit as our *Comforter*—a descriptive name revealing an important facet of his personality.

Crisis Reveals Character

Physically and spiritually bankrupt is honestly how I (Quin) felt as I was starting to write this book to encourage other women to seek the Holy Spirit's help when they feel engulfed by life's circumstances.

I was propped up in bed watching television with my right leg in a cast, my broken foot throbbing painfully. Television Bible teacher Joyce Meyer was expounding on James 1:2-3: "Consider it all joy... when you encounter various trials; knowing that the testing of your faith produces endurance" (NAS).

The phone rang. My husband's doctor called to report he wanted to schedule LeRoy for two needed surgeries within two weeks, to be followed later by his second hip replacement. Our daughter's wedding was waiting to be sandwiched in between. I had never been bedridden except for childbirth and during recovery from one surgery. But now, almost a prisoner in my bed, I was having to "count it all joy" because God was working endurance in me.

I found it hard to pray, except to cry out, "Lord, please speak by your Holy Spirit and call intercessors to stand in the gap for our family today."

Endurance is not listed as one of the fruits of the Spirit but patience and longsuffering are. "Patience is how you act while you wait," the teacher cautioned as I lay there glued to the TV. "Wherever you are in your life, God is training you for the next step. So enjoy where you are now on the way to where you are going."

I almost laughed in mockery. *Enjoy?*

Then she added, "Crisis reveals character. Character isn't formed in a crisis, that's when it is exhibited." It was painful to admit, but this crisis was revealing some areas in my character that I wasn't very proud of.

"Holy Spirit, I need you," I would pray. "Let me feel your presence."

Making Choices

The Lord showed me that I had some choices. I could put on "the garment of praise for the spirit of heaviness" (Is 61:3), or I could continue to drown in self-pity. The Holy Spirit was willing to be my comforter in this crisis, but I had to open my heart to him and cooperate with his work in me. Here are some scriptures I meditated on during my crisis:

> Beloved, do not be surprised at the fiery ordeal among you, which comes upon you for your *testing*, as though some strange thing were happening to you. (1 Peter 4:12 NAS, italics mine)

> Casting the whole of your care—all your anxieties, all your worries, all your concerns, once and for all—on Him; for He cares for you affectionately, *and* cares about you watchfully. (1 Peter 5:7 TAB)

> But if any of you lacks wisdom, let him ask of God, who gives to all men generously and without reproach, and it will be given to him. But let him ask in faith without doubting; for the one who doubts is like the surf of the sea driven and tossed by the wind. (James 1:5-6 NAS)

While we definitely believe that miraculous physical healings do happen in response to prayer, we also recognize that healing is often a process—usually a painful one. It's always aided by prayer, which helps us yield to what the Holy Spirit is wanting to do on the spiritual level while we mend on the physical level.

Because recovery takes time, we easily lose patience with the process. But if we are going to minister to others in their crises, it helps to have been there ourselves. Even when we are walking in the power of God's Spirit, we will go through trials and testings and attacks from Satan from time to time. In the midst of every pain, time of suffering, or personal dilemma, God will come with power to deliver. But we must invite him, then allow him to work in his own way and in his own timing.

Looking back over the past several months, I am thankful my husband has come through five surgeries successfully. And I can now walk, though a bit unsteadily. Friends helped with our daughter's wedding and cooked and cleaned and prayed for me. I kept writing on this book—with the laptop computer—even while propped up in bed. God did intervene to minister to my anxiety and pain, despite my impatience and inner struggles.

God's There Even in Our Heartache

Ellen, a grandmother, kept a journal of her experiences of finding the Holy Spirit's comfort during an extremely hard trial. It began the day her daughter, Karen, gave birth to a son with Down's Syndrome. She allowed us to share these excerpts:

Our grandson Jason was born today with possible Down's Syndrome. It felt like the wind was knocked out of me. Unreality. Denial. Hope. Reality. Peace. This world has no guarantees. God's plan and purpose is standing, despite what feels like a mistake. Many phone calls from friends with prayers—this has been our support and will be. I held him and he looked so normal. Our faith is being proved genuine like gold refined. He is a gift, for however long we have him. He will find a special place in our family....

God will give us *"treasures of darkness, hidden riches in secret places"* (Is 45:3). These verses were comfort and insight about our little Jason. Also: "We are hard pressed on every side, *but not* crushed; perplexed, *but not* in despair; persecuted, *but not* abandoned; struck down, *but not* destroyed" (2 Cor 4:8-9). I call these my *"BUT NOT"* verses.

Praying tonight that this suffering will not be wasted. That we will receive the treasures of this darkness. It occurred to me today that there are two ways to see any issue—50/50— negative or positive. We have to choose to be positive, or we'll be sucked into a pit.

The Holy Spirit has been faithful to help me, of course. Thank you, Lord, for this chance to stretch some more in your direction. To trust you when I cannot understand. Help me get my eyes off people and myself, and on Jesus and his eternal long-range view. He has the telescope. I have a chance to see how God sees people. Not by how much they can do, say, write, contribute. He loves us—me—Jason—just because we're people, made to reflect his glory. Jason and others like him offer me—us—a chance to be compassionate and loving, not mean, narrow, bigoted, or selfish.

As a postscript to her journal, Ellen wrote us:

This experience caused my faith to enlarge. All during Jason's first year of life, the Lord highlighted verses about *seeing as he sees, speaking as he speaks, doing what he does.* Using God's eyeglasses. He's enlarging my range of vision. Everything around me changes, but God's law and himself are more sure than any law of physics. More unchanging. The same yesterday, today, and forever. I can be the same— like him—stable, grounded. When I'm not full of life and peace, I know I'm not spiritually minded (see Romans 8:5-6).

You may not be going through exactly the same situation as Ellen, but applying her way of looking at God and people using "his eyeglasses" may help you get a different perspective on your circumstances.

More Dependent Upon God

We've talked to scores of women who have moved to another city, state, or country because of their husbands' jobs. Some look on it as a sore trial; others believe they were led by God. Pamela is one such wife.

After prayer, she and her husband left the church staff where they'd been for years to move to a smaller city in another state. A large Christian ministry had offered Wayne a job in the area of his college major. Feeling this was God's direction to them, they put their house on the market and headed west before the place sold.

Just as they were about to unload their belongings and move into a rented house, they learned Wayne's job offer was cancelled due to company cutbacks. How could this fit with the idea God had led them to make the move? Instead of making a U-turn and heading back, they decided to stay and trust God to help them find jobs.

Pamela worked part-time as a nurse, and Wayne took any job he could get as a plumber. They became active in a local church and enrolled their children in school. They had to deal with the frustration of a job that evaporated and a house which hadn't yet sold. But they also struggled with their disappointment in friends they had previously known who now lived in their new community. Not that those friends did anything wrong. Just that Pamela's expectations of their friendship were different than the way things worked out.

"I had to learn that relationships were not the basis of my identity," she said. "God did a work in my heart and showed me that my identity is in Christ—not in friends. He knew what was best for us. In the midst of our difficulty, I became more dependent upon God, and less on people."

Finally Wayne and Pamela's house sold and they were able to

buy another one in their new city. Their children are growing up in a healthy environment with lots of recreational opportunities available.

"We have made many new friends. The adjustments have been painful, but we have experienced God's faithfulness and his direction."

Wayne now has a full-time job using his talents and training to the utmost, and Pamela has cut back her hours to spend more time with their children. All their expectations weren't fulfilled, but they found a new security in God.

Sometimes we expect friends to meet our needs. Or the new job with its promised income to be our source of supply. Yet the Lord wants to prove himself as our best friend as well as our provider.

God Is Always on Time

God *can* and *does* bring intervention in the lives of his children. The women whose crisis stories we've shared now have victory testimonies. Today, on the other side of their testings, they give God the glory and praise for the way he strengthened, comforted, and taught them. Most are now helping others through crisis situations.

You've heard the saying: *God is never early and he is never late.* We are the ones who get impatient and insist on our own willful timetable.

God does intervene but not always as we anticipate. Rather, he chooses to move in unexpected and surprising ways. Usually he's been preparing us all along for his divine intervention.

Peggy, a single mom with three children, thought from time to time about remarrying. But she prayed, "God save me from myself so I don't marry the wrong man."

After being single for ten years, when her children were in their teens and early twenties, she said she reached a place where she finally "let go of a goal of having to be married." In her single years she'd learned to trust God as her provider.

He'd given her jobs in sales—a top position with one of the leading apparel manufacturers in the industry—when she wasn't even qualified. "It was God's favor, and his sending people into my life to train me in business areas I knew nothing about," she says.

When Peggy had saved enough to allow her to stay home with the children, she quit her job and spent two years as a full-time mom. During this time she would often pray in tongues eight hours a day.

"I didn't get to that place overnight; God led me to a prayer group with seasoned intercessors. When I wanted to quit I'd say no, if they can do it, I can do it. Prayer—especially praying in tongues—became a way of life for me. It taught me how to allow the Holy Spirit to flow through me. For instance, after praying this way for awhile, he would give me a word for myself or someone else. For four years I held prayer meetings in my home where others could come to pray."

Peggy's sister, living in another state, kept wanting her to meet a special friend, Frank, who was a successful businessman and a single father. But it never worked out. For four years they tried to get together. Finally, one fall the two met when Peggy was visiting her sister.

After two dates, Frank proposed marriage. As soon as he asked, Peggy says she heard the voice of the Holy Spirit say "Yes." Then she responded "Yes" quite loudly. Just two months after they met, they were married. That was seven years ago. Frank is a wonderful father and grandfather for his adopted children and their children. He highly supports Peggy's ministry, which is growing each year as she travels, speaking and teaching others how to pray.

God did save Peggy from herself and kept her from marrying the wrong man. She waited, willing to remain single. Then Frank came into her life—a man who far surpassed any expectations she ever dreamed of.

Obedience Isn't Always Easy

Holly and her husband left their denominational church shortly after receiving the baptism of the Holy Spirit, desiring to be more free to experience the gifts of the Spirit. Then about twelve years ago, she believed the Lord was speaking to her: *"Go back home—return to your roots."* She and her husband prayed and said, "Lord whatever you have for us to do there, we'll do it."

It wasn't easy, but out of obedience they rejoined their former church. However, the pastor really didn't accept her. She kept praying. A new pastor came. First she was asked to teach a women's Bible study, then invited to make worship banners and lead a group of intercessors. Women would show up at her front door asking for prayer. Often they'd have problems keeping them in bondages—through occult involvement, addictions, or stemming from abuse. She read up on the roots of these bondages, so she'd have biblical keys to set them free. Over several years of such ministry, she saw many women miraculously changed and delivered as she prayed. Then two years ago she got a phone call from her denominational headquarters asking if she'd be willing to be trained and certified to teach on the dangers of the occult.

"Here was an opportunity to teach spiritual warfare in my traditional denomination, because I had obeyed the voice of the Lord to go back," she told us. "I get invitations from all over the south. The Holy Spirit gives me wisdom to know how to pray for people with these problems, and also how to teach other believers that they too can minister in this way. Some of the people I minister to have physical illness due to bondage and oppression. When they are set free, their illnesses leave."

His Intervention May Include Healing

God's intervention often includes healing. It did for Freda Lindsay, co-founder of CHRIST FOR THE NATIONS in Dallas, Texas. As a young bride she was diagnosed with tuberculosis in both lungs. The doctors ordered one year of bedrest. Her husband Gordon was a traveling evangelist and she knew he needed her by his side. When he learned the doctor's diagnosis, he said, "This is not the will of God for *us*. The devil is trying to destroy my ministry and to take your life."

Gordon began to quote scriptures on healing, insisting it was the will of God to heal his wife. In the meantime, Freda searched her heart and asked God to forgive her for every sin she thought she might be guilty of. After several hours of prayer she says, "I felt as though I had had an internal bath. Nothing between my Lord and me. I knew I was ready to be healed.

"So together we prayed. Gordon leading out in a strong, clear voice, cursing the devil and asking the Lord to heal me in Jesus' name. I was agreeing with him. So with that as a declaration of my faith, I arose from the bed, declaring I was healed. Nor did I consult my feelings, for had I done that I would have stayed in bed. No feelings came at first. But back and forth I walked, praising God and thanking him for healing me, while Gordon shouted with me. After a few minutes I did feel stronger. For some fifteen or twenty minutes this went on. Then, feeling a little weary, I climbed back into bed, only to arise a few minutes later and proceed again to thank God for my healing."[1]

In less than two weeks she helped her husband pack and they were on the road again as evangelists. The doctors and her family still didn't know whether she would live to the age of thirty. But today Freda Lindsay has passed her eightieth birthday and is still active in the ministry of CHRIST FOR THE NATIONS.

Yes, God still intervenes with healing—sometimes miraculously, sometimes gradually. Some Christians believe in praying for the success of medical treatments or surgery to see healing come. Others believe in entering into warfare against the spirits of infirmity that hold one in sickness.

Notice that Gordon thanked God in advance (prayer) for healing his wife. He also bound the devil and his schemes (spiritual warfare). Freda did her part in asking forgiveness of her sins and moving out in faith to believe God was healing her—little by little.

We do not encourage readers who are sick to act in presumption. The above story simply reports on the faith and actions of a Spirit-filled couple who believed they were acting on God's Word. We advise you to seek a word from God before you assume you are to take a particular action toward healing.

Authority and Power

Dr. Charles Kraft, professor of anthropology at Fuller Theological Seminary, writes in *Christianity With Power*:

> I'm afraid the way we usually refer to the part we are to play in God's healing ministry is very misleading. We usually speak of "praying for healing." But prayer is ordinarily understood as petition or asking. We would not label what Jesus did when he ministered to people as "prayer." He usually commanded the condition to be well (Lk 4:39; 5:13; 7:6-10 implied), or the spirit to leave (Lk 4:35), or the winds and waves to be still (Lk 8:24), or the person being healed to do something in faith (Lk 5:24; 6:10; 7:14). Sometimes he would touch the person (Lk 5:13). At other times people would touch him and be healed (Lk 8:44; Mt 14:36). *He prayed before he did his deeds, not during them* .... I believe we are to imitate Jesus and take authority as he did.[2]

Dr. Kraft brings up an important but controversial issue, concerning *praying* for healing and *doing warfare* against evil hindrances. Because there are two thoughts on healing in Christian theological circles, we give his explanation:

> *I see an important difference between praying and taking authority.* Though we often use terms like "pray for" or "pray over" to label what we do when we minister, in actual ministry I find

myself more likely to *command* the condition to leave than to ask God to relieve it. In Luke 9:1, we read that Jesus gave the disciples power and authority to drive out all demons and to cure diseases. I believe it is the taking of authority over the condition on behalf of Jesus, rather than the need to ask Jesus to heal, that is our primary function in this kind of ministry.

There is an important place for prayer, of course. Nothing gets done without it. But the prayer comes primarily in preparation for the ministry. Before we ever attempt to minister healing, we need in prayer to assure both God and ourselves that what we desire is his will not ours. In prayer we attempt to line up our will with his and to ask God to minister to the person who seeks his help. In prayer we confess our sin and unworthiness and ask for his power to defeat the enemy in the coming encounter. Without such preparatory prayer, we have no authority and power. Then, at the start of the ministry session, we pray to request God's presence, power, and insight.[3]

Prepared for an Emergency

Gretchen's story is an illustration of the effectiveness of spiritual warfare in healing. She is a Spirit-filled woman who for more than ten years has made a practice of spending time with the Lord each morning, getting what she calls her "manna for the day." From her daily reading she would take one verse on which to meditate during the day, usually memorizing it.

One morning when she was particularly rushed, she wrote down the verse that was her "manna" for that day and slipped it into her purse. She was almost late getting to the three-mile road race where her husband Jack was to run. But halfway through the event, she got word that Jack was having difficulty breathing. She knew from past experiences he was having a severe asthma attack.

He was rushed to the hospital's critical care unit where, after an hour of aggressive therapy, doctors reported that Jack was near total respiratory arrest. Death was a very real possibility. "I felt like yielding to panic, or just sitting down to have an uncontrollable cry," Gretchen reported. "Then suddenly I remembered my manna verse. What had God said to me that morning? I couldn't remember! I quickly whipped it out of my purse and began to read aloud...

> With long life will I satisfy him and show him my salvation. (Psalm 91:16)

"I realized I had a choice," she said. "Either listen to the doctor with his 'possible death' report, or believe and stand upon the Word of the Lord."

She chose the latter. First she rebuked the devil: "Satan, I know your plan is to steal, kill, and destroy, but you will not have my husband. God's Word to me is true, and Jack will live and have long life. I refuse to believe an evil report."

Then she began to praise and worship God right in the critical care unit of that hospital. She continued declaring God's Word over her husband. Not only did Jack live; today he is a coach at a Christian school, and together he and Gretchen believe he will enjoy a long life.

We agree with Dr. Kraft when he says the one ministering in power needs to start where Jesus started—with the infilling of the Holy Spirit (see Luke 3:22). He goes on to say:

> Jesus did no signs and wonders before that point in his life. When Jesus ascended to heaven, he told his disciples to wait until the Holy Spirit would come upon them and empower them before they went out to minister for him (Luke 24:49, Acts 1:8). They, like Jesus, were not to do signs and wonders or witness to God's loving concern for humans *until* they were working under the complete control of the Holy Spirit.[4]

Dealing with Grief

Eventually every Christian will experience some form of Gethsemane—illness, pain, disappointment, betrayal, tears.

Perhaps yours is grief. If so, you can identify with our friend Marsha who lost her sixteen-year-old son, Aaron. Though she had known the Lord and his empowering Holy Spirit for some time before her son died, she went through a painful five-year journey to wholeness. She recalls the experience:

> Right after Aaron's death I was numb. About six weeks later the shock lifted, and the full brunt of our loss hit hardest. For me, it was six months before I could function normally in mundane things, like managing my checkbook.
>
> My husband and I agreed to allow ourselves time to grieve, no matter how long it took or what form it took. But we determined not to blame each other. I needed friends to stay close. The weight of grief would lift if a friend would just sit and listen. After I'd spent time talking about my son, then we would talk about things of the Lord.
>
> I often had to bind a spirit of self-pity from attacking me. Also, I'd bind the devil from taking advantage of my emotional frailty. I'd find myself praying that unhealthy grief would not overwhelm other members of our family, for we had a son and daughter yet living.
>
> On the fifth anniversary of his death, I had a vision in which I saw myself placing Aaron in my Heavenly Father's lap and leaving him there. That somehow brought closure to the grieving process. During such a period of grief things in you change; you "grow up" so to speak. I received the Lord's comfort, but the loss of my son will always be a painful reality in my life.

Today Marsha helps other parents walk through their own grieving processes. She says, "No matter how long you've known the Lord, at times of grief, you must throw yourself on the promises in his Word to walk through your personal valley."

Though you may not have experienced the same level of anguish as Marsha, you may be grieving over the loss of a job, a broken relationship, or betrayal by a friend, a spouse, a child, or a parent. Grief is painful, no matter what its source.

Christian counselor Dr. Larry Crabb reminds us, "Disappointment is a chronic reality for the self-aware Christian." He goes on to say, "The longings of our heart must be faced. The disappointment of our soul must be experienced. Only then will we learn to pant after God in eager anticipation of His coming, when every desire will be forever satisfied."[5]

In times of heartache, you can know that Jesus identifies with you for he was "a man of sorrows, and familiar with suffering" (Is 53:3). You are not alone. God has not failed you. He sees the end from the beginning—a much larger picture than you are able to comprehend. And he will build endurance in you, helping you to mature in your faith even when you don't understand (see James 1:4).

Ask the Holy Spirit to comfort you in your heartache, and guide you into God's plan for your future. Sometimes it's a long time between a promise from God and its fulfillment, but he will deal with us in wisdom and compassion. Trust his timing. Don't allow seeming delays or disappointments to keep you from believing his promise.

Angelic Intervention

Of course, supernatural intervention can include far more than healing, or spectacular guidance. Quin's Aunt Betty, now in her eighties, has been walking in the Spirit for almost forty years. She carries on a continual daily dialogue with the Lord, often praying in tongues for hours on end.

A widow for more than three decades, Aunt Betty has learned to depend on the Lord as her husband. One day while driving alone on a freeway in southern California, her radiator blew. She maneuvered the car to a stop and continued praying in the Spirit. Then in English she prayed, "Lord, send me help." She had barely spoken that prayer aloud, when a young man stopped, told her to lock her car, get her purse, and come with him. Trusting that God truly had sent him, she got into his car and rode with him to a nearby repair garage where she could arrange for a tow truck to pick up the car. "I looked to thank him and he was gone," she told Quin. "But I've never questioned that it was the Lord who sent him. You see, I depend on the Holy Spirit to pray through me every day."

Do angels drive cars on Los Angeles freeways? Aunt Betty firmly believes they do!

Not the Way They Planned

If in your walk with the Lord, when you trusted and prayed, God intervened in ways unlike what you expected, could you trust him to know what's best? Cybil shared her lesson learned with us.

As soon as her husband, Doc, finished his medical residency, Cybil packed up their four children and a few belongings and followed him to the mission field in Latin America.

"We believed the Lord wanted us to be medical missionaries. We truly had heard his direction. So we went. There were absolutely no medical facilities where we settled and since Doc's specialty was delivering babies, he was very busy. We also did evangelistic work encouraging the native people to start churches so new converts could get further training."

Doc and Cybil had only been on the mission field for eight months when his parents visited them. On their second day there, Doc's father died of a massive heart attack. They brought him back to the States for the funeral. After it was over, they kept trying to go back to the mission field, but there seemed to be roadblocks.

They didn't want to quit as failures. But were they to return? They asked God to give them a sign, an answer.

It came soon in the form of a letter from a doctor they'd

known while in Latin America. He warned them there was too much unrest and that it was unsafe for them to return. In fact, he was very emphatic that they should not come.

Considering it their sign from God, Doc settled in the States to practice medicine. Twenty years later he went back to the area where they had spent only eight months as medical missionaries.

"God was so good to allow Doc to see how the native men had become pastors and the work of the Lord was flourishing," Cybil told us. "Also, he was pleased to learn that shortly after we left, the government realized the need to build clinics and hospitals for its people. He heard such good reports about how effective our short stay there had been. God's timing is not always ours and his assignments aren't always easy. But looking back, you can see he will move you to a place for only a short time to accomplish what he wants, though you may feel you either failed God or didn't fulfill the assignment."

God's intervention is often not what we expect. He will sometimes surprise you with extraordinary events that the Bible calls signs and wonders.

Signs and Wonders

I (Quin) had an amazing experience when I attended a gathering in Seattle in 1988, where leaders of several women's ministries met for prayer. About a dozen of us were in a hotel room praying when suddenly the room began to shake. I had been standing with my hands on the wall, praying and crying out to God in my prayer language. When I looked around I watched furniture creep across the floor.

Carolyn, one of our group, picked up the phone and called the desk. "Are we having an earthquake?" she asked. "Our room is shaking."

"Of course not," the desk clerk replied curtly. "Maybe you are next to the laundry room and the machines are causing your room to vibrate."

Carolyn and I stepped outside to investigate. This room was between two other guest rooms, not adjoining the laundry room. We were experiencing an event similar to that recorded in Acts 4:31: "After they prayed, the place where they were meeting was shaken. And they were all filled with the Holy Spirit and spoke the word of God boldly."

Our group had been interceding for an event to begin the next day called Leadership 88, when several hundred women would gather to hear Bible teacher Joy Dawson teach on what it takes to be a woman leader.

If we thought the room shaking during our prayer meeting was supernatural—which it was—the way the Lord shook most of us over the next two and a half days was even more miraculous. As we heard teaching on repentance and restoring of relationships, the leaders of key organizations washed the feet of leaders from other groups. Repentance and forgiveness led to the healing of relationships and promises of prayer support between the leaders.

The morning after our room-shaking experience, a man staying at the hotel told a woman in our group, "I had a strange thing happen last night—just one wall of my room shook." His room, we learned, was next to our "prayer room." This confirmed to us that we had really experienced a supernatural outpouring of God's power.

Biblical Intervention

The Bible is full of stories about God's intervention in the lives of his handmaidens as he brought about his plan in the fullness of his timing. Consider these biblical women who experienced God's intervention:

- Hannah cried out to God, and had her barren womb healed for her Samuel to be born, followed by other children (see 1 Samuel 1-2).

- Elizabeth, old beyond childbearing age, gave birth to John the Baptist, then said, "The Lord has done this for me... he has shown his favor and taken away my disgrace among the people" (Lk 1:1-25).

- Faithful old Anna praying in the temple for years was granted her desire to see the Messiah before her death (see Luke 2:36-38).

- A woman bent over for eighteen years, crippled by a spirit, was immediately healed when Jesus saw her in the synagogue on a Sabbath, put his hands on her, and said, "Woman you are set free from your infirmity" (see Luke 13:10-17).

- The widow of Zarephath, who gave her oil and meal to make cakes for Elijah, experienced a multiplication miracle as God replenished her small supply so that it lasted through the long drought (see 1 Kings 17:8-24).

- Esther, Deborah, Naomi, Mary, and Martha—all of them saw God intervene to bring about his plan and purposes.

Yes, the Holy Spirit can and does bring about God's supernatural intervention, but not always as we might expect.

PRAYER

Lord, help me see as you see, speak as you speak, and act as you act. May I learn to trust you when my situation looks utterly hopeless. Remind me that for me to declare something hopeless is to say I have a helpless God. Nothing is impossible with you. You are bigger than any mountain I may face.

Thank you for your precious Holy Spirit who is my comforter. Lord, comfort and walk with me through my pain, disappointment, betrayal, sorrow, and suffering. Hide me in the shelter of your wings; there I will seek refuge. Thank you for helping me trust that you have the bigger picture of my life's circumstances. I choose to cast my cares, worries, and disappointments on you, for you care for me. Help me yield to your intervention and lay aside my expectations when they are not from your heart. I pray in Jesus' name, Amen.

EXERCISE

1. Recall other Biblical examples of God's intervention.

2. Write down times God "came through" for you and praise him for his supernatural workings.

3. Write down promises he has given you that have not yet come to pass. Some may be special words he's given you or Bible verses that he has quickened to your heart.

TEN

❧

Walking in the Spirit

If we live in the Spirit, let us also walk in the Spirit.
Galatians 5:25 NKJV

Spirit-filled living means a moment-by-moment reliance upon the inner guidance of the Holy Spirit. The Greek word for *walk* here literally means "to walk in line with." It's an "exhortation to keep step with one another in submission of heart to the Holy Spirit, and therefore of keeping step with Christ," writes W. E. Vine.[1]

How can a woman learn to recognize the Spirit's prompting in walking the path God has chosen for her? What are the daily disciplines that clear the way for the Spirit to work, and the pitfalls that keep us from walking in the Spirit?

The name of a unique woman comes to mind whenever we think of one who has learned to walk in the Spirit consistently: Bobbye Byerly. This scripture verse describes her: "She opens her mouth with skillful and godly Wisdom, and on her tongue is the law of kindness...." (Prv 31:26 TAB).

Bobbye's life gives evidence today that she truly walks in the Spirit with love and discernment, bringing healing to many hurting women. The truth is, at one time she was a broken, hurting woman herself.

Born to a mother in a mental institution and shifted from home to home as a child, she married while a teenager. After giving birth to three sons, caring for a semi-invalid mother-in-law, and being wife to a man who seemed married to his job, she was ready for divorce. But a question on a plane trip changed her direction.

Do You Know My Jesus?

"What's troubling you?" the Japanese man sitting in the plane seat beside her asked.

"Oh, nothing that God can't handle," Bobbye answered. She knew her answer was the truth, but it was not truth for her at that moment. She was headed for Houston to attend her father's funeral. Gazing out the window through the clouds she tried to clear her mind of the problems at home, and prepare emotionally for this family gathering where she would see all the aunts who had helped to rear her.

The man from Tokyo pressed further. Finally Bobbye told him she was en route to her father's funeral. "I can see you are hurting," he said. "Do you know my Jesus?" Turning to stare out the window again, Bobbye couldn't even answer him. But his question haunted her.

Here she was, an American woman who had been in church all her life, being asked by a Japanese man whether she knew Jesus. Masking her pain, she made it through the funeral and flew back home to New Jersey, but she couldn't shake that question.

Six weeks later, with her marriage crumbling and making plans to leave her husband, she went to see her pastor for a final session of counseling. During the discussion, Bobbye blurted out the question that had troubled her for weeks: "Do I know Jesus?"

Suggesting that she needed to seek an answer on her own, the pastor left her in solitude. During the next six hours while closeted in that church office, long after the pastor had gone, Bobbye had an experience with the living Lord. To this day—thirty-four years later—she can't fully explain what happened. But she came out of that room knowing for sure Jesus loved her, had forgiven her, cleansed her, and imparted to her an overwhelming love to share with others.

"I'd been in church much of my life, but until that moment when I was touched by Jesus' love and presence, I really didn't *know* him," she said. "The man on the plane had planted seeds that were now beginning to sprout."

Miracle of Love

The first miracle happened as soon as she got home that afternoon. She went immediately to her semi-invalid mother-in-law, Maggie, who had lived with them for nine years.

"Mom, I love you," Bobbye said, bending over the bed to envelop Maggie in a hug.

"I know you do, dear," she responded.

"No, you don't understand," Bobbye insisted. "I mean... I *really* love you!" For years Bobbye had blamed her own unhappiness on her mother-in-law. Now she felt differently as she continued hugging her and letting Jesus' love flow through her to Maggie. The older woman got out of bed—which she seldom did—and joined in welcoming a surprised Jim home from work.

"The Lord healed the relationship between Maggie and me that day," Bobbye said. "When I told Jim I'd stay in the marriage he was glad. The Lord has so blessed our marriage since I allowed him to turn me around. Instead of escaping and going my own way, I found Jesus, and he helped me to walk in love. Later on, Jim found him too."

Bobbye soon was thanking God for another miracle. Her own mother, who had suffered for twenty-seven years with drug addictions, alcoholism, and mental illness, was also delivered. "As she confessed her sin, she was set free, and for the next four years, until her death, she was a glorious Christian," Bobbye reported.

Her three sons embraced the Lord also. In the meantime,

she had another experience—"the Lord baptized me in the Holy Spirit and I spoke in a language I didn't understand," she said. "But it was just another step in bringing me closer to Jesus."

The Seeds Bear Fruit

Today Bobbye is U.S. National President of Aglow International, a women's ministry organization, and she serves on their international Board of Directors. She also serves as prayer leader for the intercessors' team of the Spiritual Warfare Network, as well as working with several other missions and prayer organizations, including A.D. 2000.

Bobbye's been to six continents in recent years reaching out to hurting women.

I (Quin) have had the privilege of ministering with her in hospitals, orphanages, and churches in Russia, watching her bring reconciliation on Native American reservations, and seeing her touch women in cities and hamlets all across our country. Both Ruthanne and I have served on intercessory teams Bobbye has led in prayer efforts in Korea, Argentina, California, and Colorado.

Indeed, that seed planted by a Japanese man during a plane ride has borne fruit that touches thousands of people around the world.

What is Bobbye's secret? The discipline of spending much time in her prayer closet. Hours and hours of prayer, praise, and worship, and waiting on the Holy Spirit for direction in making nitty-gritty decisions. It's as though every breath is one big prayer—her Lord is that close. Her example inspires us more fully to enter into God's presence through praise and worship.

What Does It Mean?

What does it mean to walk in the Spirit? Pastor David Wilkerson of Times Square Church in New York City has expressed it well:

Walking in the Spirit means incredible, detailed direction and unclouded decisions. The Holy Ghost provides absolute, clearly detailed instructions to those who walk in Him. If you walk in the Spirit, then you don't walk in confusion—your decisions aren't clouded ones.

The early Christians did not walk in confusion. They were led by the Spirit in every decision, every move, every action! The Spirit talked to them, and directed them in their every waking hour. No decision was made without consulting Him. The church's motto throughout the New Testament was: "He who has ears to hear, let him hear what the Spirit has to say."[2]

Seizing an Opportunity

Walking in the Spirit means staying alert and open to the Holy Spirit's direction in everyday situations, even while on the job. Dawn is a Spirit-filled nurse who looks for opportunities to quietly share her faith with her patients in subtle ways.

One night on Dawn's shift, Trina checked into the hospital to keep from miscarrying her third child. She had been struggling with bouts of vomiting and dehydration. Dawn was assigned to help her get settled in the room and begin treatments.

In unpacking Trina's suitcase, Dawn pulled out a paperback version of the Bible called *The Book* and put it on the bedside table. "That's my favorite book, too," she said with a smile.

"It *used* to be my favorite," Trina answered glumly.

"Well, maybe God's giving you some time to spend with him while you're in here for rest and recuperation " Dawn responded.

"Yeah, maybe," Trina said, looking out the window.

"Can I pray for you?" Dawn asked, after checking her vital signs and filling in her chart.

"OK," Trina agreed, showing no enthusiasm.

Dawn prayed for healing for the mother and the baby—especially that Trina would have strength to carry it to full term. "Lord, make yourself known to Trina in a powerful way during these next few days," she finished.

After that brief encounter, Dawn's nursing shift changed, and patient and nurse didn't see each other again.

Six years later Trina attended a women's conference where Quin was teaching. Dawn was there to be Quin's prayer partner and lead a worship chorus to open the session.

Afterwards Trina rushed up to Dawn. "I recognized your voice when you began to sing today!" she said. "You're the nurse who prayed for me to carry my baby to full term. That was six years ago, and today we have a healthy, beautiful daughter."

Dawn stared at her. "What about you? You must have had a change of heart to be attending this Christian women's conference."

Trina brought Dawn and Quin up to date on her life since that eventful day. "After you prayed with me and left the room, I rededicated my life to the Lord," she said. "I confessed that I'd made a big mess of my life, and I asked God to help me clean it up.

"I received the Holy Spirit after getting home from the hospital, and I tried to live a godly life before my husband, Rick. He was a professional musician, playing rock and roll music in bars and clubs. Before my experience in the hospital, I had prayed, 'Lord, change him.' But after I prayed, 'Lord, change me,' as I begged God for Rick's salvation, he agreed to go to church with me one Sunday night."

Rick later asked one of the men at church what it means to accept the Lord. Once it was clearly explained, he committed his life to Christ, as well as his musical abilities. Now he helps with the music and the young people at their church, and has become a full-time associate pastor.

"God worked powerfully in my life and my husband's life after you prayed with me in the hospital that day," Trina told Dawn. "Now we have a vision for building a facility to help young women in crisis situations, and God has already provided the land for the project."

Miracle Answers to Prayer

We never know what seeds we are planting when we obey the nudges of the Holy Spirit, and most of the time we don't know the result. What a blessing when he occasionally gives us a glimpse, as he did Dawn in this case, to encourage us to continue obeying his voice as we walk in the Spirit.

Dawn now works in a hospital neuro-critical care unit where only patients with traumas from gunshot wounds, strokes, car accidents, and similar situations are admitted. She prays for each of her neurological patients at times when she is the only one in the room.

"I pray aloud and tell them how Jesus loves them and died for them; then I tell them how to receive him as their Savior. I say, 'Even though you can't speak, in your heart you can speak to God and tell him you want to accept Jesus.' Since hearing is the last sense to go, they often can hear me even when they appear to be in a coma. Besides, I am speaking to their spirits, where the most important response takes place."

One of Dawn's recent patients was a twenty-three-year-old single mom who'd had a head-on collision while driving to work. She was admitted to Dawn's critical care unit with head and other multiple injuries. Listed in critical condition, she was bleeding to death.

"Her death certificate had already been written out and was waiting to be signed by the coroner," Dawn reported. "Two Christian family members, two chaplains, and I gathered around her bed, laid hands on her, and prayed for her healing."

The woman didn't die as the doctors expected, but she was still critical. In the days that followed, other prayer groups and intercessors were alerted.

"At every opportunity I would walk into the room and speak the Word of God over her: 'Live; do not die. You will live to see the goodness of the Lord in the land of the living!' Her mother had told me she was a Christian."

Three weeks later the woman was transferred out of the critical care unit to rehabilitation. The bleeding had stopped and there was no more brain swelling. She went through therapy to restore strength to her muscles and learn to walk again. But the fact that she lived was a miracle in answer to prayer.

"Though my job is emotionally and physically draining, I believe I'm an answer to someone's prayers—maybe a spouse, a mother, or grandmother—when I'm able to minister to a patient," Dawn shared. "Of course we don't always see recovery in answer to prayer; sometimes I am there when they leave this life. I may be the last one to hold their hand or speak words of comfort. I know it's where God wants me to be for now."

A.B. Simpson wrote:

If we would walk in the Spirit, we must obey Him when He does speak.... If we will be still and suppress our own impulses and clamorous desires, and will meet Him with a heart surrendered to His will and guidance, we shall know His way (see Psalm 25:9).

... Let us be sensitive to His touch, responsive to His whisper, obedient to His commandments, and able ever to say, "The Father hath not left me alone; for I do always those things that please Him" (Jn 8:29).[3]

Depending on the Holy Spirit

Mary Elizabeth's story illustrates how a mother of five went from a place of quiet defeat to one of complete dependence on Spirit-led living. She shares in her own words:

Over the years I've found that if I have a word from the Lord—whether from the Bible itself, or one that he speaks to my heart—I can make it through just about anything.

I have five children, including a set of twins. Because I was concerned about providing for their college education, I fully planned to return to my career in nursing to help with those hefty tuition bills. I had worked in nursing for four years before my first child was born, but every time I determined to go back to work, I'd find I was pregnant again. I decided to wait until the first child was almost ready for college to return to work.

As that time drew near I was seeking the Lord one day. He spoke very clearly to me that I was to give him my desire for a nursing career, and stay at home to mother my children and keep them covered with prayer. I felt he showed me that each child had a special calling, and he wanted me to teach them and pray for them to enter fully into his plan for each one. The Lord said if I would do this, he would *fully provide* for them to go to college.

I can't say that I accepted this word joyfully; it was a big disappointment to give up nursing. But after grieving and pouting for a few days, I agreed to obey his word to me. Within a few months my longing for a nursing career was gone. Now I wanted nothing more than to stay at home, pray for my children, and teach them everything I could about God's Word.

During my oldest daughter's senior year in high school, we began investigating colleges and asking the Lord which one he wanted her to attend. Though the finances looked impossible, she chose a small Christian college which would help her prepare for her dream of being an overseas missionary. She had some scholarships, but there remained a balance of $4,300 to be paid in a few short weeks.

I knew the Lord had promised *full provision*, and he is always faithful to his Word, but storms of doubt and guilt seemed to rage all around me. We barely had money for groceries, much less her college tuition. My daughter was becoming increasingly frustrated and upset about it— wondering if I had *really heard from the Lord at all.* I would retreat to my room to seek the Lord, read again the Word he had given me years before, and try to regain strength for the battle. But I *knew* God had spoken to me.

About ten days before the trip to take my daughter to college, my husband was in an accident. The long trip was too much for our damaged car, and the insurance settlement was too low to buy another car. The picture looked dark indeed, but faithful friends stood by me in prayer as I kept trusting in God's word to me.

A few days later we learned our daughter had won a $4,300 grant for her first year of college. This exact amount which we lacked was being sent directly to the college. Then we learned the insurance company of the man who hit our car decided to cover the rental on a minivan so we could transport our daughter to college. Every need was met.

Since then we've had three children in college all at the same time, and God has faithfully provided for each one as they prepare to serve him in missions. God is true to his Word, and I know he'll provide for my last two children when their time for college comes.

Standing on God's Promise

For Mary Elizabeth, getting a word from God meant giving up her own ideas of how her children would get an education, and then standing firm in her trust that God's promises were "Yes" and "Amen" for her and her family.

When she first got the Holy Spirit's direction to give up her desire for a nursing career, it took awhile for her to adjust to the idea. Then the Word was tested.

It would have been so easy to say, "I must not have heard from God at all—I just thought I did. I'd better get busy and figure out how to borrow the money or go out and earn it." But Mary Elizabeth was living and walking in the Spirit day by day, relying on the inner guidance of the Holy Spirit. She held onto God's promise, and he was faithful to fulfill it.

God Opens Doors

Six months after Marie had received the baptism of the Holy Spirit, she felt a strong urge from the Spirit to enroll in a particular Bible school in another state. Though she had no savings, she felt led to fill out the application and trust God to open doors if she was to go. After she filled out an application she realized she had to have a physical exam.

She approached a doctor in the hospital where she worked and asked him to give her the physical, explaining why she needed it. "Please don't mention to anyone that I have applied for Bible school," she told him. "I might not be accepted and I can't afford to lose my job."

He looked at her and said, "Marie, if you get in, I will pay your tuition for however long it takes." She was accepted! He paid all her school costs except for food during her two years there.

"The Lord gave me a word of knowledge that this doctor had a call on his life and he never fulfilled it," Marie told us. "I believe the doctor felt he was seeing God's call come to pass by paying my way to school to prepare for ministry. He was actually a backslidden Christian. But this was God's way of supplying what I needed for Bible school."

God's Leading Is Sometimes Subtle

Sometimes we are led by the Holy Spirit and aren't even aware of it at the time. Think about times in your life when you've had that experience. You went about your daily life— which at times seems so hum-drum—faithful in your daily disciplines. Then bang! God moves supernaturally. One day you realize God has accomplished that extraordinary thing you've been trusting him to do.

Sometimes when you have asked for something—like changing your tendency to worry for an attitude of simple trust—it may take a crisis to make you realize he has indeed given what you asked for. That's why it is good to daily ask the Holy Spirit to guide our thoughts and actions. The Scripture says, "The steps of a good man are ordered by the LORD, and he delights in his way" (Ps 37:23 NKJ).

Often in our prayer time together my husband and I (Quin) will remind the Lord of that verse and add: "Lord we are asking and expecting you to order our steps today. Thank you."

Other Ways the Spirit Leads

The longer you walk in the Spirit, the more intimately you will get to know the Lord. As you study the Bible he may highlight by the Spirit things he wants you to do. Things you had never thought of in relation to walking with him—such as:

1. Proclaiming the Word of God around your house or as you walk your neighborhood. God's Word will not return void. (See Jeremiah 3:12; 11:6; Isaiah 55:11; 61:1.)

2. Dancing—either in the privacy of your own home or on a sacred worship team in your church. One woman who for several years has been using dance as a medium to praise the Lord told us, "We are created to fellowship with our Creator and praise him. When I dance I am worshiping him with my feet, fingers, toes, muscles, bones, lungs—my whole body. Dance—or creative movement—is the embodiment of worship. I celebrate what he's done for me by dancing in gratitude. The Word says, 'Let them praise his name with dancing and make music to him with tambourine and harp. For the LORD takes delight in his people;\...' (Ps 149:3,4a)."

3. Taking up the tambourine to do warfare (as a brandishing

weapon; see Isaiah 30:32). "I am laying judgments on the enemy as I go through my house, beating my tambourine," one intercessor told us. "As I do, I am disarming principalities and commanding them to flee from my house. I may go to my daughters' bedrooms, and shake and beat the tambourine while aloud I rebuke the spirits of terror and fear that the enemy tries to put on them. I proclaim that no evil will come near our dwelling. Then I sing praises and sometimes dance while using my tambourine like Miriam in the Old Testament."

4. Laughing and shouting for joy. God is restoring laughter to his people. Read the Psalms for many examples of rejoicing in the Lord. Also, women of today are discovering the shout—which can be an acclamation of joy or a battle cry when doing spiritual warfare.

5. Fastings. There will be times in your Spirit-walk when you will want to abstain from food. Jesus said "when" you fast, not "if" you fast in giving instructions for fasting (see Matthew 6). Times of fasting can yield answers to prayer, direction from God, strategy for warfare, new revelation of Scripture, a closer walk with the Lord, a humbling of self, healing of body, mind, and emotions, and deliverance from evil spirits. If you have medical problems, you may need to follow a modified or partial fast. Some intercessors feel it is beneficial to take a private prayer retreat during a fast.

6. Weeping sometimes accompanies deep intercession. It may come from a spirit of identification or brokenness in the one praying, or during times of intense repentance.

Finding Balance

Walking in the Spirit also requires finding the delicate balance between *work, rest, worship,* and *play*. In his book *The Rhythm of Life,* Richard Exley encourages Christians to put life's priorities in proper perspective in these four areas.

Meaningful work gives our lives definition and purpose. Yet, without a corresponding amount of rest, even creative or spiritual work becomes tedious. Work without rest inevitably produces burnout. Worship and play must then be added to the work/rest cycle to produce the Abundant Life. Rest restores our physical vitality and renews our emotional energies. In restful solitude, we forget the world with its pressing demands for a while and remember who we are. Worship goes a step farther and enables us to forget ourselves for a while and remember Who God is. It puts everything into perspective.... The final element in the rhythm of life is play. It relieves the tension and gives balance to the whole of life. By divine design, we need it all and we ignore this rhythm at our own peril.[4]

Finding balance is a challenge for busy women. But we encourage you to take inventory. Ask the Holy Spirit to help you balance your times of work, rest, worship, and play.

One of our friends who is a traveling minister recently went away to fast and seek God for direction. She reported that for the first three days about all she did was sleep and sit quietly before the Lord. She didn't realize how exhausted she was until she became still. In making herself learn to play again, she would take walks around the ranch where she was visiting, watching the deer and wild rabbits and enjoying God's creation. She'd become so wrapped up in work that she'd neglected to rest and play.

Can God Really Speak to Me?

God has used our friend Beth Alves to teach hundreds of spiritual warriors guidelines on how to hear from God. In her book *The Mighty Warrior* she says:

Drawing near to the Lord opens the door for Him to fellowship and communicate with you.... The Lord speaks to you through the person of the Holy Spirit (Ezekiel 36:27; John 14:16-17).

... One way to know whether you are hearing the Holy Spirit is to use this test: Does the voice gently lead you in a direction, or is it commanding and harsh? God's voice gently guides and encourages, giving you hope (Psalm 18:35; Isaiah 40:11; James 3:17). GOD LEADS, SATAN DRIVES (John 10:4). God convicts, Satan condemns and brings guilt (Psalm 8:1-2). God woos, Satan tugs hard. When God speaks, He does not use fear to motivate. If fear overcomes you, it is the enemy speaking, not God (2 Timothy 1:7).[5]

Beth gives these guidelines to hearing the voice of God:

- Bind the voice of the enemy.
- Submit your own will and reasoning to the Holy Spirit.
- Turn off your own problems.
- Give your undivided attention to God's Word.
- Limit your own talking.
- Write it down. (The Spirit of the Lord will speak to you through impressions or pictures in the theater of your mind. When this happens, write them down.)
- Don't argue mentally.
- Wait upon the Lord for the interpretation.
- Don't get ahead of or lag behind the Holy Spirit.
- The Holy Spirit sometimes speaks through music. Listen.
- Pay attention to your dreams. Write them down. Not all dreams are of God.
- Don't be afraid of silence. Don't be upset if you don't hear anything when you pray. The Holy Spirit may just want you to worship the Lord.[6]

Divine Appointments

How God longs for us to walk in line with his plans and purposes for us day by day. But we can only do that effectively if we have an intimate relationship with him. If we don't know him well enough to recognize his voice, we can't possibly communicate. In this narrative, Jesus compares himself to a shepherd and us to his sheep:

> He [the shepherd] calls his own sheep by name and leads them out. He walks ahead of them; and they follow him, for they recognize his voice. They won't follow a stranger but will run from him, for they don't recognize his voice. (John 10:3b-5 TLB)

Ordinary women like us can be guided by the Holy Spirit continually if only we allow him to be our beacon. My (Quin's) elderly Aunt Betty is forever praising the Lord aloud. "Thank you, Jesus, for this parking spot," she'll say. "Thank you, Jesus, that you cleared the traffic ahead so I wouldn't have to drive in congestion. Thank you, Jesus, that today you will show me where I can get yarn to make baby blankets for the unwed mothers' home."

Just the other day Aunt Betty felt the Lord instructed her to go to a certain store for her yarn. When she inquired about a particular type she needed, the clerk said the store didn't carry it. But another customer standing nearby overheard the conversation. "I have some extra yarn just like you described," she told Aunt Betty. "Here's my phone number. Call me and I'll give it to you—no charge. I'm glad you're making blankets for the unwed moms. I'm working to save babies from abortion."

"That was a divine appointment!" Aunt Betty said in telling me about it on the phone. "The Lord guides my steps every day because I ask him to. Since I live alone, I talk to the Lord continually. I spend my time praising him instead of concentrating on my aches and pains. I fully expect him to keep giving me divine appointments, just like he did in the fabric store."

God Can Do Anything

Pat, a young, single career woman, believes as strongly as Aunt Betty does that God can do anything. She tells him so everyday. Recently when she felt the Lord was leading her to buy a house, her realtor could find nothing suitable in her price range. Pat already had gone through the procedure of acquiring a house loan, but she didn't have the house to buy.

"God, you have a house out there for me," she told the Lord in prayer one day. "I am tired of looking. You can do anything, so I'm trusting you to find it."

Right after that a new customer came into the furniture store where Pat worked, wanting to look at sofas. She told Pat she was fixing up her house to sell. As they talked, Pat became interested in the details of the house and was excited to learn her customer was a Christian. The woman insisted that she come and look at her house which she'd just put on the market.

"I kept telling her it sounded way out of my price range," Pat told us. "But a couple of days later I arranged for my realtor and five of my praying friends to go with me to inspect the house. As soon as I walked in and saw the marble floors, three bedrooms, two large living areas, a spacious yard, and colors that would match my furniture, I knew this was the house. It was just right to hold my prayer group and Bible study crowds."

"Let's make an offer," her realtor suggested. Pat and her friends prayed, and one of them came up with the same amount for an offer as the amount her realtor had in mind. "God, if you want me to have this house, you will have to move to get the offer accepted," Pat told the Lord. "I can't pay more than the figure you showed me."

Not only was the offer accepted, but exactly one week from the time her customer told Pat about the house, she signed the contract to buy it. The expiration of Pat's apartment lease and the date the owner of the house needed to move coincided exactly.

Don't Miss This Adventure

"One of the unusual things is that for two years I had been driving up and down that street going to and from work, always praying in tongues," Pat said. "Never did I imagine I could live on such a street in such a house. Nor did I know what I was praying for as I prayed in the Spirit all those mornings—I just felt I was interceding for something on God's heart. An amazing thing about this is that the woman I bought the house from used to own several abortion clinics in the city. But she received Christ, got rid of the clinics, and is now serving the Lord. She was praying for a Christian to buy her home and use it for God's glory. Our intercession made the way for us to meet by divine appointment, in God's timing."

Now that she has her own home, many people come for teaching, worship, Christian fellowship, and ministry. We know from personal contact that our friend Pat truly walks in the Spirit, spending quantity and quality time with the Helper himself.

We concur with David Wilkerson's advice:

Give much quality time to communion with the Holy Spirit. He will *not* speak to anyone who is in a hurry. All of God's Word is about waiting on Him!... Wait patiently. Seek the Lord and minister praises to Him. Take authority over every other voice that whispers thoughts to you. Believe that the Spirit is greater than these, and that He will not let you be deceived or blind. Be willing to set your heart on Him as Jacob did—and not let go until He blesses you![7]

If we want to walk in the Spirit, we will learn to know his voice with distinct preciseness. And listen for his direction. We will be willing to spend whatever time it takes in his presence to accomplish it. Walking in the Spirit is an adventure you won't want to miss!

PRAYER

Thank you, Lord, for the gift of the Holy Spirit that enables me to walk in victory through every difficulty. Forgive me for the times I've failed to wait for your direction and walked in my own strength. Thank you for your faithfulness in redeeming my mistakes. Lord, help me to tune out the clamor of the world, the flesh and the devil, and listen for your still, small voice. Speak by your Holy Spirit and direct my path, leading me to the divine appointments of your choosing. I pray that my walk and my words will honor and glorify you, in Jesus' name, Amen.

ELEVEN

❧

Avoiding the Pitfalls

I know that after I leave, savage wolves will come in among you and will not spare the flock. Even from your own number men will arise and distort the truth in order to draw away disciples after them. So be on your guard! (a portion of Paul's farewell address to the Ephesian elders)

Acts 20:29-31a

If our Spirit-filled walk with the Lord is comparable to taking a journey, then we would be wise to learn in advance about possible pitfalls which could deter us. The New Testament contains countless warnings against deception, pride, greed, unforgiveness, wrong motives, selfishness, disobedience, and many other traps to guard against.

Paul's farewell address to the Ephesian elders in Acts 20:17-35 is primarily concerned with deception and division wreaking havoc in the church after his departure. The *Spirit-Filled Life Bible* says this address, in its written form, "became a permanent word of warning and instruction to all the Gentile churches that Paul had established."[1]

Every one of us is susceptible to falling into pitfalls. Scripture tells us, "If you think you are standing firm, be careful that you don't fall!" (1 Cor 10:12). But when we remain open to the Holy Spirit, he is faithful to warn us against the traps lurking in our path.

Identifying Pitfalls

As we have traveled, taught, and prayed with thousands of women in many cultures, we've discovered some of the major pitfalls they encounter in their spiritual walk. Here is a partial list, followed by discussion regarding some of them:

• Deception (Matthew 24:4-5, 11, 24-26; 2 Corinthians 11:3, 14)
• Dividing the body of Christ (Ephesians 4:2-6)
• Manipulation (2 Corinthians 4:2)
• Praying soulish prayers (James 4:1-3)
• Holding grudges (Ephesians 4:26-32)
• Presumption (Acts 5:1-11)
• Missing God's timing (Acts 16:6-15)
• Unbelief (Hebrews 3:12-4:2)
• Personal ambition; not making room for others' gifts (Philippians 2:3-4)
• An untamed tongue (James 1:26; 3:9-10)
• Not obeying the word God gives you (Luke 6:46-49)
• Gossip; taking up someone else's offense (2 Corinthians 12:20)
• Operating out of your mind—not open to Spirit (1 Corinthians 2:12-14)
• Lack of vigilance (Ephesians 6:18; 1 Peter 5:8)
• Spiritual pride (1 Corinthians 4:18-20)
• Dabbling in New Age or other godless philosophies (Colossians 2:6-8; 2 Timothy 4:3-4)

Now let us examine some of these traps more carefully.

Guarding Against Deception

Laying yourself open to deception is: *Trusting everyone who says he or she is a Christian, or believing every "word from God" that others give you; also, accepting as true that which is not biblical.*

We are to "test the spirits" (1 Jn 4:1) as we ask the Holy Spirit for discernment—then heed his warnings. Sometimes deception is so subtle we become easy prey to it unless we remain open and sensitive to the Holy Spirit's leading.

Doris, a Spirit-filled Bible school graduate, was both deceived and manipulated, though at the time she didn't recognize her dilemma. A woman she greatly admired who was well established in a Christian ministry told her one day, "I feel that God wants you to work with me."

When Doris prayed she couldn't get a clear direction from God one way or another. Finally, as the woman kept pressuring her with promises for ministry opportunities, Doris gave in and moved to another city to join this woman's staff. However, the ministry wasn't able to pay her a salary, so she had to take a part time job to cover living expenses.

Soon the woman was controlling almost every aspect of Doris' life, constantly telling her what to do. Still she didn't discern the deception and control. A turning point came when they went on a ministry trip to a city where Doris had previously lived, and some of her friends came to the meetings.

"One friend approached me and advised me to leave that ministry; she and my other friends could see the control," Doris told us. "But I was offended by her advice. I found out later that four of those who had seen me at the meeting met together afterward and prayed for two hours that my eyes would be opened. One woman then talked to me again and said my personality had changed. I was not even the same person I used to be because of this woman's control over me.

"Not only did I listen this time, but it was as if the blinders came off my spiritual eyes. Now I could see that the woman I worked for was manipulating me. I went back and packed my things, returned to where I'd previously lived, and got another job right away."

What lessons did she learn? Doris says, "I learned I must always receive the Word of the Lord for myself, and not listen to what other people say is God's will for me. That is one safeguard against being deceived. Wait on the Lord no matter how long it takes; if you don't feel you have an answer, then don't move. Be a God-pleaser and not a man-pleaser. I was glad I had friends who cared enough about me to pray and then confront me with the truth of my deception."

Deception comes in many forms: believing teachings that are contrary to Scripture, listening to voices other than the Holy Spirit's, mixing truth with error, etc. One of the most subtle deceptions is the New Age movement. According to author Phil Phillips:

> The New Age philosophy is a blend of Eastern religions (something of a western variant of Hinduism and Buddhism), occultism, and evolution theory. It claims that all religions are equally valid and all are merely different paths back to God. Its key tenet is that all human beings are divine—all are gods. We get in touch with our "god-ness" through altered states of consciousness.
>
> A new twist in the movement has opened the door for many Christians to be sucked in. Whereas Christians could once readily identify and reject New Age teaching because of the emphasis on reincarnation, the new emphasis on angels and the afterlife has a much closer alignment with what many Christians *think* they have grown up believing.[2]

How we need to test philosophies and teachings with the Word of God to avoid the pitfall of deception! Just because a book, film, or teaching mentions angels does not mean it's presenting biblical Christianity. What a new-ager calls an "angel" or "spirit guide" is most probably a demonic spirit (see 2 Corinthians 11:14). Even seemingly harmless "good luck charms" or other artifacts from ungodly cultures are included in the things Scripture warns against in Deuteronomy 7:25-26 and 18:9-14.

The Apostle Paul gives us this warning:

> Do not deceive yourselves. If any one of you thinks he is wise by the standards of this age, he should become a "fool" so that he may become wise. (1 Corinthians 3:18)

Being Aware of the Counterfeit

We agree with Dr. Peter Wagner's warning not to confuse spiritual gifts with counterfeit ones.

> I wish it were not true that Satan and his demons and evil spirits are real and actively opposing the work of the Lord. Jesus himself said, "For false christs and false prophets will arise and show great signs and wonders, so as to deceive, if possible, even the elect" (Mt 24:24). Jesus also speaks about those who prophesy and cast out demons in his name, but who, in reality, turn out to be workers of iniquity (see Matthew 7:22,23). I do not doubt that Satan can and does counterfeit every gift on the list. He is a supernatural being and he has supernatural powers.... Of course, Satan's power is limited and controlled.[3]

Listening to the Holy Spirit

I (Quin) learned, as our friend Doris learned, the importance of listening to God rather than people, especially those who might want to control you. Once two women gave me a "word" that was radically contrary to what I believed the Lord had shown me.

About two years after I had received the baptism of the Holy Spirit, someone sent me a brochure about a Christian writer's conference in Dallas at CHRIST FOR THE NATIONS Institute (CFNI). I had never heard of this Bible school, but I was hungry to learn more about Christian writing. My husband felt it was an excellent opportunity for me, and Mom offered to come watch our three children while I was gone. I was excited with the prospect of flying alone from Florida to Dallas to hear lectures by well-known Christian authors.

Two nights before I was to leave, two women I barely knew, who sometimes came to a prayer group I attended, knocked on the door. One told me in no uncertain terms, "We have a word from God for you. He is not pleased with you leaving your family and going off to that school. Besides, you don't need that training. Stay home. Don't go. Thus says the Lord," she finished, in a very demanding voice.

At first I was upset and confused. Was I making a big mistake? Was I doing the wrong thing to leave my family for five days? When I told my husband what these women had said, he calmed me by saying, "Don't pay any attention to them. You and I and your Mom agree it is God's will. Go enjoy yourself, meet people, and learn lots."

At that conference I met Ruthanne Garlock, who has now been my co-writer for six books. I learned much from teachers like Marjorie Holmes and Jamie Buckingham. Other women in ministry I met there became close friends, including Beth Alves.

I also became so sold on CHRIST FOR THE NATIONS Institute that I recommended it to our family. All three of our children, after getting college degrees, went to Dallas and graduated from CFNI. Two of them met their mates there. Finally, after retirement LeRoy said it was his turn for Bible training. So for almost three years we lived on the CFNI campus enjoying some of the best Christian fellowship and training I could imagine. In that time span Ruthanne and I lived only one block apart and wrote two of our books together. Today as a result of his Bible school experience, LeRoy serves as an associate pastor in our church in Colorado Springs.

You tell me, who heard from God? My so-called "friends" who tried to stop me from going to Dallas? Or my husband and I? I shudder to think of the blessing my family and I would have missed had I not attended that conference. Thank God for a husband who is an encourager and who hears God, too.

Avoiding Manipulation

Manipulation is *receiving a prophetic word, then trying to "make it happen" instead of waiting for God's timing and God's way. Or attempting to control others' lives through a "word from God," finances, or intimidation.*

Usually a personal word of prophecy will confirm something the Lord is already speaking to you about. If the word seems contradictory to what he has shown you, it's important to ask the Holy Spirit for clarification and confirmation.

One biblical example of manipulation is Sarah, the woman who remained childless until the age of ninety when God fulfilled his promise and gave her a son. But as she grew impatient with the years of waiting on the promise, she insisted her husband, Abraham, have a child by her maid Hagar. This produced Ishmael, a rival to her own son Isaac born several years later. One Bible scholar says Sarah became "the woman who made a great mistake." Though she manipulated the circumstances to achieve her goal, yet God redeemed her mistake. The New Testament says of her, "she judged Him faithful who had promised" (Heb 11:11 NKJV). Although we may pay the price for falling into manipulation—as Sarah did—we can admit our mistake and receive God's forgiveness. He lovingly forgives and restores us.

Praying Soulish Prayers

Praying soulish prayers is *asking for what you want or think is best, rather than praying Spirit-led prayers.*

More than one woman has admitted to us that she told God what man she wanted for her husband, manipulated circumstances to make it happen, only to discover that her soulish desire was not God's choice. Now she's living in the misery of the consequence, begging God for deliverance.

Soulish praying is a form of manipulation. And that is closely related to witchcraft—using sorcery to try to control people and circumstances. People who pray soulish prayers very often mean well, but usually are so blinded by their own reasoning or desires they don't realize that their prayers are not submitted to the Holy Spirit.

Here are a few examples:

- A mother who tries to intervene in her children's lives through self-centered prayers. Such a mom tries to control everything from a child's choice of a career or a mate to meddling in her adult child's child-rearing methods or financial affairs.

- Trying to dictate to God how you want your prayers answered and getting angry when his answers don't meet your expectations.

- Trying to control church leaders through selfish prayers, intimidation, gossip, or withdrawing financial support.

Holding Grudges

Holding grudges means *harboring unforgiveness against a person for any reason—but especially when you're misjudged by those who belittle or dispute your spiritual experience.*

June is an intercessor whose strong interest is praying for the most spiritually needy nations of the world. Hundreds of intercessors, June included, have taken prayer journeys to some of these nations to pray "on site with insight."

Recently in her church, a visiting minister began speaking against this type of prayer ministry, calling it a waste of time and money. "They should use that money for evangelists to preach the Word on television, and we could get the people in those countries saved," he declared.

June went home from the meeting feeling greatly offended, as angry responses to the man churned in her mind. "I knew I couldn't go to bed feeling that way, so I began to pray, asking the Lord to show me this man's heart," she said (see Ephesians 4:26-27).

"The Lord revealed that he had been hurt by a group of intercessors, and this made him prone to judge them unfairly. I had to choose not to carry a grudge toward this minister—it wasn't easy, but I knew it was necessary. I repented for my own heart attitude toward him. Then I repented on behalf of the intercessors who had hurt him. The Holy Spirit changed my heart, and as I felt empathy for him I wept over this man in intercession."

Looking back on the experience, June said she realized anew the danger of holding a grudge in a situation like this—especially toward a spiritual leader. "I would've become a target for the enemy had I not dealt with my heart attitude in this matter," she said. "It's important—especially for intercessors—to pray Psalm 51 and Proverbs 3:5-7 every day, and to guard their hearts to avoid this pitfall."

We are to model Jesus' prayer, "Father, forgive them, for they do not know what they are doing" (Lk 23:34). Being misjudged by others—even well-meaning friends—is part of the price of spiritual progress. Forgiving them is our protection.

Missing God's Timing

We may hold back, reluctant to do what God is leading us to do, or run ahead of the Holy Spirit instead of moving at his bidding. Either way we miss his timing.

Dee Eastman is one of my (Quin's) prayer partners who has helped me understand God's timing more clearly. She compares it to God moving in seasons, and, of course, the winter season of our life is the hardest.

"God may be setting us aside for a period of learning from the Holy Spirit," she said. "It is preparation for the spring. If we don't have the winter of dormancy, we won't be prepared for springtime with its blue skies, bursting blossoms, new life, and fresh breezes."

Last year during a "winter season" in my life, Dee and I met for prayer on Tuesday mornings whenever I was able. We would read and meditate on these verses:

> See! The winter is past; the rains are over and gone. Flowers appear on the earth; the season of singing has come, the cooing of doves is heard in our land. The fig tree forms its early fruit; the blossoming vines spread their fragrance. Arise, come.... (Song of Solomon 2:11-13)

Dee kept praying for springtime to come, and indeed it did. I just had to wait for God's timing. We must become willing to wait. On the other hand, when God tells us to do something we must not delay our response and miss his timing and his best for that season of life.

One young woman clearly heard God's instruction to go to a mission training school. Reluctant to give up her job and friends at the moment, she waited several months. "When I finally obeyed and went, it was a difficult experience. I asked the Lord why I was so frustrated—after all, I had obeyed him. He impressed on me that I had missed his perfect timing in going. But that experience has made me more obedient and more sensitive to God's timing."

Obeying Is Better Than Presuming

Presumption is *thinking that a given opportunity or a "word" is from God; or acting on a word without the Holy Spirit's direction.*

Just because a job or ministry opportunity seems more exciting than your present occupation, doesn't mean it's God's choice for you. Seeking godly counsel and asking the Lord for confirmation is always a good idea. I (Quin) have known women whose husbands—without seeking God—moved them across country for an optional job promotion, but with heartbreaking results to the family.

Denise is a Spirit-filled young woman who learned the

danger of presumption from her own near-mistake. Believing the Lord was leading her to encourage and pray for patients in a nearby hospital, she dressed in her best outfit one morning, dropped her child off at "Mom's Day Out," then headed to the hospital, Bible in hand. But as she entered the building she felt a check from the Holy Spirit.

Stopping in the hallway to ponder this sudden about-face, Denise then felt the Holy Spirit directed her to go to the hospital chapel.

"Lord, I got dressed up and came here to minister to people one-on-one," she prayed under her breath. "If you just want me to pray privately, I could do that at home." Nevertheless, she obeyed the hunch and went to the chapel.

To her surprise, she met the hospital chaplain whose office adjoined the chapel. Having had little experience with hospitals, she didn't know the institution even had such a staff person. When she mentioned why she had come that morning, the chaplain tactfully explained that unauthorized persons were not allowed to do this kind of work.

"However," he quickly added, "we do have a two-week training program we offer twice a year for laypersons who are interested in chaplaincy ministry. A class is starting next week, and I'd be happy to enroll you for the course."

Now Denise understood why the Lord had led her to visit the hospital that particular week, and then redirected her steps once she got there.

"Had I gone ahead with my own plan and not obeyed the Holy Spirit, I could have been devastated," she shared. "The hospital chaplain would have stopped me from what I was doing, and I would have felt like a total failure. Also it would have caused me to doubt that I could hear the Holy Spirit at all, and the enemy would have assaulted me with guilt. I learned a valuable lesson in obedience that day."

Not Believing

Unbelief is *failing to embrace God's promises and to stand in faith for victory when circumstances become difficult.*

Women who succumb to this pitfall may pray, but in their hearts fail to believe God will hear and answer *their* prayers. The important thing is to be sure your prayer of faith is in agreement with God's will. Jesus said, "If you remain in me and my words remain in you, ask whatever you wish, and it will be given you. This is to my Father's glory, that you bear much fruit, showing yourselves to be my disciples" (Jn 15:7-8).

Some years ago Dick Mills told a woman in one of his meetings that God's promise in Luke 19:9 was for her—that her entire family would be saved. In his ministry newsletter he wrote about the results:

Maria wrote to us off and on as it began to happen. She had twelve children. When three of them gave their lives to the Lord, she wrote and shared her joys with us. Several years later two more came in. Three years went by and another one was converted. Every time we got a letter from Maria another child had been won to the Lord. Her last letter came ten years after she had received her first promise [for] family salvation. All twelve of her children ultimately came to the Lord. When you are dealing with delays in answers to promises the Lord has given you there are some encouraging things to consider: A delay is not a denial.... Better to have a slow answer than no answer.[4]

What would have happened if she had moved into unbelief and said, "Impossible—all twelve of them?" Instead, Maria received God's promise as her own, and combined faith with her prayers for her children.

Taming the Tongue

You have an untamed tongue if *your speech is motivated by selfishness, desire for revenge, or lack of understanding.*

Scripture says, "The tongue of the wise commends knowledge, but the mouth of the fool gushes folly.... The tongue that brings healing is a tree of life, but a deceitful tongue crushes the spirit" (Prv 15:2,4). With our tongues we can bring division and corruption, or we can speak life and hope. To speak or pray in other tongues requires yielding our tongues to the Holy Spirit. It is equally important to be yielded to the Holy Spirit when we're speaking a known language.

Have you ever had a so-called "spiritual" friend who uses her tongue to criticize almost every spiritual leader she hears in a meeting or on television? She finds one statement she doesn't agree with, labels the speaker a heretic, then phones her friends to explain his "error."

When we see behavior or hear teaching by another believer that raises questions, we should first speak to God about our concerns, then address the issue with others as the Holy Spirit leads. The Bible is explicit in its instruction:

Do not let any unwholesome talk come out of your mouths, but only what is helpful for building others up according to their needs, that it may benefit those who listen. And do not grieve the Holy Spirit of God, with whom you were sealed for the day of redemption. (Ephesians 4:29-30)

"Sometimes we talk so inadvisedly," says author Lance Lambert. "Beware what you say about a message you have heard, about someone else's testimony or their walk with the Lord, or about a work of God, even if these things are outside your present understanding."[5]

Getting Rid of Spiritual Pride

Spiritual pride is *considering oneself more knowledgeable, more doctrinally correct, or more spiritually gifted than others—the opposite of true humility.*

If we heed Paul's warning not to think of ourselves more highly than we ought, the Holy Spirit will protect us from spiritual pride (see Romans 12:3). But be aware that the enemy works in subtle ways to ensnare believers with this pitfall. Sometimes spiritual pride masquerades as humility, so we must be sensitive to the Holy Spirit.

About fifteen years ago I (Ruthanne) began receiving requests to speak for various women's groups, but almost always would devise excuses for declining the invitations, or pass them on to a friend. The times I did agree to go I experienced great fear and insecurity and felt the Lord was expecting me to function in an area for which I was not gifted. And besides, I reasoned, there are lots of other better-qualified women out there.

So I prayed about it—or thought I did. Actually, what I called "prayer" really was my complaining to God. The Holy Spirit revealed that my problem was false humility, a devious form of spiritual pride. I confessed that I was resisting the Holy Spirit's assignments for me—and that my primary fear was of failing to live up to my own self-imposed standard—and genuine repentance followed. I've learned that when I humbly obey the Lord and rely upon him, the Holy Spirit never fails to enable me to speak, to write, or to do anything else he may call me to do.

Since each of us is made in God's image, we are to show respect for one another, but we must avoid putting certain ones on a pedestal because of their high-profile gifts. Whether we're in an exalted position or a lowly one, we should keep a biblical perspective of ourselves and of others.

Jesus, knowing who he was, where he had come from, and where he was going, exhibited great humility when he took a towel and washed the disciples' feet (see John 13). Then he said, "I have set you an example that you should do as I have done for you. I tell you the truth, no servant is greater than his master, nor is a messenger greater than the one who sent him. Now that you know these things, you will be blessed if you do them" (Jn 6:15-17).

I (Quin) was recently at a large gathering of Christians where the Spirit of God was moving, and manifestations were taking place unlike any that people in the audience had ever experienced. The pastor made these two piercing statements:

"Can you be humble enough not to criticize what you don't understand—and go home and mirror it against the Word of God?"

"Folks, you can't stop a move of the Holy Spirit, but be careful that you don't miss it yourself."

That should have dealt a death blow to any spiritual pride in the meeting.

Avoiding Personal Ambition

Personal ambition is *being so intent on using your spiritual gifts—or on enjoying the services for selfish reasons—that you "church-hop" until you find a place to your liking.*

God's plan may be for you to "bloom where you're planted." As you cultivate the fruit of the Spirit and submit to his leading, he will cause your gifts to make room for you (see Proverbs 18:16).

When her husband's job required a relocation, Martha complained that they were moving to a dry and desolate place because Ray insisted on going to their traditional church. Since she'd been Spirit-filled a long time, she yearned for a fellowship where she could get spiritually refueled every week with powerful worship and teaching. Though Ray said she didn't have to go with him, she reluctantly decided she'd do it for the sake of their relationship.

Her personal ambition for finding another congregation

changed dramatically one day. "When I got quiet before the Lord and allowed him to speak to me, I felt he showed me that there were three people in this church he wanted me to intercede for. It was like an assignment from the Lord—the very reason for my being there."

Martha soon realized all three individuals were key leaders in the church, but were not even born-again Christians. She and Ray prayed for them over a period of time, then they established a friendship with them and consequently led all three to accept Jesus as Savior. Two of them received the baptism in the Holy Spirit, and, today, one of those two has a very effective ministry to the homeless.

Martha and Ray moved again shortly after this—as if they had completed the Holy Spirit's assignment for them in that church. But it was an important lesson for her.

"Don't think the Holy Spirit can't use you in a dry, hard place," she shared. "If you have a vision of what he wants to accomplish through you—and if you obey, you will be surprised. A word from God literally is like water in a desert. When he calls a Spirit-filled Christian to a dry place, the anointing of intercession is automatically upon you. It can be one of the most loving, intimate, and fruit-bearing chapters of your life."

Operating by Human Reasoning

Gerry had been a Spirit-filled Christian for some time, involved in counseling and praying with troubled women, when she herself went into depression. This dark cloud had been over her for about two months when a close friend died.

"I was feeling no emotion whatsoever over the death of one I loved, so I knew something was wrong—I needed counseling," she said. "I had been trying to find a solution for all these people I was praying for, and giving them counsel. But often they ignored my counsel, then when their problems got worse, the devil would harass me. I didn't think it was possible for the devil to assault my mind—but this subtle attack had gone on for two months before I began to realize what was happening."

When she went to talk to her pastor for help, he first prayed for her, then commanded the tormenting spirits attacking her mind to loose her. Then they both prayed in tongues as they felt the release of the Holy Spirit.

"Gerry, if you find yourself constantly thinking about how to solve everyone's problems, you should pray in your prayer language," he instructed her. "One of your problems is that you always try to reason things out and find a solution—keeping your mind busy with matters which belong to God. This is putting your trust in your mind, not in the Lord. Finding the solution is the Holy Spirit's job."

Then he explained that her mind was sometimes *too* fruitful—which is why praying in tongues is a good idea. He reminded her of the scripture, "For if I pray in a tongue, my spirit prays, but my mind is unfruitful" (1 Cor 14:14).

Gerry walked out of the pastor's church office and the dark clouds of depression seemed gone—the sky was blue. But immediately the enemy began telling her that her deliverance was only temporary. "No, devil, you aren't winning the battle in my mind!" she declared aloud. Then she again prayed in tongues. The depression completely left her and has not come back in six years. Gerry now uses her prayer language more often than ever before in intercession and praise. "It also serves me well when a case of 'busy brain' makes it difficult for me to get to sleep at night," Gerry said with a laugh. "My prayer language is a gift from God that helps me avoid this pitfall."

Overcoming Division and Disunity

One of the enemy's schemes is to divide the body of Christ and prevent our coming into unity. Satan is actively trying to prevent the answer to this prayer Jesus prayed: "May they be brought to complete unity to let the world know that you sent me and have loved them even as you have loved me" (Jn 17:23b).

Almost all the pitfalls discussed in this chapter contribute in one way or another to disunity. When the Holy Spirit helps us on a personal level to avoid these pitfalls, this works toward overcoming division on a corporate level. We can help be a part of the answer instead of the problem when we obey this instruction:

> Be devoted to one another in brotherly love. Honor one another above yourselves. Never be lacking in zeal, but keep your spiritual fervor, serving the Lord. Be joyful in hope, patient in affliction, faithful in prayer. Share with God's people who are in need. Practice hospitality. Bless those who persecute you; bless and do not curse. Rejoice with those who rejoice; mourn with those who mourn. Live in harmony with one another. Do not be proud, but be willing to associate with people of low position. Do not be conceited. (Romans 12:10-16)

Avoiding Pitfalls

We asked several seasoned intercessors for their suggestions for avoiding pitfalls. Their suggestions include:

- Be yourself. When you are giving a prophetic word, if loud is not your nature, don't shout.

- Practice. When you think you have a word, don't be afraid to give it and don't be intimidated by other people. If you do make a mistake be humble enough to admit it. One friend reported that over a five-year period she often sensed God was giving her a word during public meetings, but she would just wait on the Lord. When someone else spoke the prophetic word aloud it confirmed what God had shown her. "During that process I was learning to trust that indeed I was hearing from God, and this made me more confident to speak out publicly," she said.

- Wait. Don't give the Lord an agenda, or try to predetermine how and when he will move. Be willing to wait for him to speak to you, then allow him freedom to move through you.

- Honor God. We need to be filled every day with the Holy Spirit, walking in his presence and power. Many Christians talk about God or Jesus but they ignore the Holy Spirit. We need to honor him and invite him to be a part of our everyday lives.

- Feed on God's Word and good Christian teaching by listening to wholesome tapes and worship music—even Bible-reading on tape. What you put into your spirit becomes evident in your daily walk.

- Seek guidance daily. As you begin your day ask the Lord, "What is your word for me today?" When you ask, he will often speak in various ways to give you a word or instruction for that day.

PRAYER

Lord, show me the areas of my life where I may be walking in deception, spiritual pride, manipulation, unbelief, presumption, personal ambition, unforgiveness, soulish praying, or using my tongue in an unwholesome manner. Whatever the vulnerable area is, Lord, I want to be open and humble before you. I give the Holy Spirit permission to correct me and be my Helper. Show me how to cooperate with the Holy Spirit's work in my life to avoid these traps, and keep my feet on the path that follows your footsteps. I ask this in Jesus' name, Amen.

EXERCISE

1. Review the list of pitfalls at the beginning of the chapter, and read all the scripture references given.

2. Write down the items you feel the Holy Spirit is alerting you about in your own life, and steps you can take to avoid these pitfalls.

3. List additional pitfalls which you feel could be problems for believers in general, and find scripture references pertaining to them.

Proclaiming the Good News!

*The Lord gives the command; The women who proclaim the
good tidings are a great host.*

Psalm 68:11 NAS

Spirit-filled women have a message.

That message—*He is alive!*—has the power to change people
and circumstances in families, neighborhoods, cities, and
nations.

"Speech is the woman's ministry," says our friend, evangelist
Dick Mills. "Verbal expression goes with a woman's calling—
women and words go together. It was women who proclaimed
the good news about the destruction of Pharoah, the death of
Goliath, and the resurrection of Christ."

In researching the above verse (see Psalm 68:11) Mills
checked eighty different Bible versions. Many of the most
respected translators and commentators understand the original language to say it was *women* who proclaimed the news of
victory. Here is a sampling of various interpretations given to
the Hebrew word which often appears as *company* or *host* in the
verse:

Young's: A host of female proclaimers.

The Vulgate: Women evangelists.

Matthew Henry: Prophetesses.

Ellicott: Women who bring the divine utterance.

Delitzsch: The evangelists like Miriam and Deborah shall be
a great host.

A Praise Processional

One Old Testament example of a woman who did this is Miriam, Moses' sister. According to Mills' research, when news came of a military triumph, women would form praise processionals to celebrate with victorious songs of thanksgiving. It was just such a processional which Miriam led after God miraculously delivered the Israelites from Egyptian bondage:

> Then Miriam the prophetess, Aaron's sister, took a tambourine in her hand, and all the women followed her with tambourines and dancing. Miriam sang to them: "Sing to the LORD, for he is highly exalted. The horse and its rider he has hurled into the sea." (Exodus 15:20-21)

Deborah is another example. She was a judge and a prophetess in Israel who had a word from God that he would deliver the enemy into their hands. She went with Barak and the army to watch it happen, then she proclaimed the news by composing and singing the victory song, which concluded:

> "So may all your enemies perish, O LORD! But may they who love you be like the sun when it rises in its strength." Then the land had peace forty years. (Judges 5:31)

Women Proclaim the Good News

When Jesus had an encounter with the Samaritan woman at the well, she hurried to her village to tell everyone, "Come, see a man who told me everything I ever did. Could this be the Christ?" (Jn 4:29). Many people in her town believed in him because of her testimony. Then Jesus himself went there and taught for two days, and many more became believers (see John 4:1-41).

Think of the story of Mary Magdalene and Mary, the mother of James, who encountered an angel at the tomb who told them, "... go quickly and tell his disciples: 'He has risen from the dead....'" (Mt 28:7). As they went on their way, fearful yet full of joy, they met Jesus himself, who told them, "Do not be afraid. Go and tell my brothers to go to Galilee; there they will see me" (v. 10).

We read that during his earthly ministry, many women followed Jesus and ministered to him. Can you imagine what it might have been like to have been in that group of "certain women" who were in Jesus' inner circle?

- A woman, Anna, had at his birth proclaimed him to be the Messiah.

- The inner circle of women followed him to the cross with many others, but were the last to remain there.

- Two devoted women were the first to come to the tomb to minister to him.

- Thus it was women who had the privilege of first proclaiming the news of the resurrection.

Jesus clearly valued women, and he elevated their status for all time by the way he, a Jewish teacher, honored them. Women also waited in the Upper Room for the promise of the Father, were filled with the Holy Spirit, spoke in tongues, and participated in the commission to "go and tell."

On the Day of Pentecost Peter reminded the crowd of Joel's prophecy:

> ... this is what was spoken by the prophet Joel: "In the last days, God says, I will pour out my Spirit on all people. Your sons and daughters will prophesy, your young men will see visions, your old men will dream dreams. Even on my servants, both men and women, I will pour out my Spirit in those days, and they will prophesy...." (Acts 2:16-18)

Lydia (Acts 16:14) was the first convert won to the Lord at the beginning of Paul's first missionary journey. She invited

Paul to her home, and he very likely preached there to Lydia's family and neighbors. Some scholars feel she was instrumental in starting the church in Thyatira, her home city.

Priscilla (Acts 18:26) was a teacher, and Phoebe (Romans 16:1) possibly was a woman evangelist. The four daughters of Philip (Acts 21:8-10) were recognized as prophetesses, and Paul spent several days in their home. In sending greetings to the church at Rome, Paul mentioned no less than ten women by name, some of whom he called "fellow workers" (see Romans 16).

Prayer and Proclamation

Women today also can be empowered by the Holy Spirit to proclaim—*go and tell*—the Good News. One criticism of Spirit-filled people is that their experience seems to put them on an emotional "high," yet has little practical impact on their daily lives. But God sends the Holy Spirit for a dynamic purpose: to propel us outward to fulfill the Great Commission.

Ready to Proclaim

Terry is a young woman whose life has changed from being angry toward God because he didn't fulfill her expectations, to sharing the Good News whenever she sees an opportunity. Recently her husband, Fred, had an invitation from the chaplain of a nearby prison where he formerly had worked, to visit a chapel service at the facility. On impulse, he asked Terry if she would like to go along, and she said yes.

"When we got to the chaplain's office, he told us it had been a very hectic week, and he hadn't had time to prepare anything for the meeting," she told us. "He asked Fred whether he had a message he could bring. To my amazement, Fred looked at me and said, 'Terry, do you have something you'd like to share?' Immediately I felt the Holy Spirit told me, 'Say yes,' so I did. It was a step of faith to believe that I could open my mouth and the Lord would fill it, but that's what happened. I shared from Scripture, then told the prisoners how God had changed my life, and they were very responsive. We were able to hug them, pray for them, and encourage them before we left."

Of course, any sharing of our faith should start with prayer. But our praying can go beyond our private prayer closets or our small groups of intercessors. Prayer can be a proclamation to our neighborhoods and cities, releasing God's word of redemption throughout the area. In their book, *Prayerwalking*, Steve Hawthorne and Graham Kendrick, modern leaders in this form of prayer, write:

Prayer walking is just what it sounds like it would be: walking while praying.

... Prayerwalking is on-site prayer—simply praying in the very places where you expect your prayers to be answered.

... Walking helps sensitize you to the realities of your community. Sounds, sights and smells, far from distracting your prayer, engage both body and mind in the art of praying. Better perception means boosted intercession.

... Walking also connects Christians with their own neighborhoods. By regularly passing through the streets of their cities, walkers can present an easygoing accessibility to neighbors. Walking seems to create opportunities to help or to pray for new friends on the spot, right at the times of great need. Some streets present risks, but vulnerability yields valuable contact with those who have yet to follow Christ.[1]

Neighborhood Miracles

Our friend Mary Lance Sisk has witnessed many miracles in the neighborhoods of Charlotte, North Carolina, since scores of women have begun prayer walks. Some of the most outstanding results are the many small neighborhood "prayer triplets" (three people praying together) being formed as the movement grows.

"I believe the key to the healing of the United States is going to be neighborhood by neighborhood, with women doing it!" she said. "Evangelism is a lifestyle of love which results from having Jesus' heart for the lost."

Mary Lance encourages women to intercede daily for their neighbors and to pray for God to raise up a prayer movement in each neighborhood. She takes literally Jesus' command to "Love your neighbor as yourself," and Peter's admonition to "proclaim the praises of Him who called you out of darkness into His marvelous light" (1 Pt 2:9 NKJV).

Walking on her street, she makes it a habit to proclaim Scripture. "Lord, we invite the King of Glory to come in. Come forth and bring your glory into this neighborhood. Release your blessing to the families here."

One of her neighborhood's most successful events is called "Meet You At The Corner." The neighbors gather on the Saturday morning before Easter for a short service declaring "He is alive." They share refreshments and fellowship. Flyers are distributed door to door—even the children come along with their parents.

"We're able to share about the resurrected Lord in a contextual way," Mary Lance said. "It's one of the best ways in the world to meet your neighbors."[2]

Before you begin prayerwalking in your neighborhood or city, experienced intercessors suggest these preliminary steps:

- Prepare your heart with the Lord.

- Evaluate your neighborhood (or city) by knowing history or layout. Don't take on too much territory all at once. For instance, Mary Lance suggests you might want to walk several streets in your neighborhood but only pick one to five families to pray for on a regular basis during your devotional time.

- Ask for his purpose and vision for your prayer walk.

- Seek God for guidance as to what Scriptures to use as you

walk. Memorize some that you can say aloud as you walk, declaring God's love for your city.

Hawthorne and Kendrick warn us:

As we look upon our own cities, we are tempted to respond inappropriately in one of two ways: either to condemn the city or to carry its sorrows. Neither way is God's way. Do not try to *carry* the sins of others so as to atone for their wrong-doing. You are a priest, not the sacrifice. Only one person is able to carry our sorrows. The Father has given this cup to Jesus alone. The opposite error is to see the doom of the city and to *condemn* it.[3]

They suggest three things a prayer intercessor must do to walk and pray for a city:

- Stand before God offering gifts of praise, especially thanks offerings.
- Stand with your city in repentance—cry for mercy (see Luke 19:41-44).
- Stand in your city, extending blessings from God's heart.[4]

Several Old Testament scriptures are key to prayerwalkers, such as: "I will give you every place where you set your foot, as I promised Moses" (Jos 1:3).

Another is based on Jeremiah 29 where the children of Israel were encouraged to seek the peace and welfare of the city where they were in exile and to pray for the city, for as the city prospered, they would also (see Jeremiah 29:7-8).

March for Jesus

In addition to prayerwalks, many cities are organizing once-a-year *March for Jesus* praise processions. These have spread worldwide as Christians in dozens of nations from different church backgrounds and cultures celebrate Jesus with exuberant praise. Their purpose is to glorify Jesus, not to protest anything. The marches include singing in unison and carrying handmade worship banners made by many women.

I (Quin) was thrilled to participate in my first *March for Jesus* in Colorado Springs. I was overwhelmed that so many Christians could gather on a Saturday morning simply to unite in lifting up banners and songs of praise to Jesus. Graham Kendrick's taped worship songs blared from the public address systems, providing us music to sing along with as we marched.

I (Ruthanne) participated in the first *March for Jesus* ever to be conducted in Israel in June 1994 while I was there on a study program. About two hundred believers made history as we gathered at The Promenade overlooking Old Jerusalem and the Mount of Olives, lifting up praises to our Lord.

In 1981, I (Ruthanne) participated in a prayer journey to China, shortly after that country began allowing visitors to come from western nations. Many others have told me their experiences of prayer walking in China around that time also. Although an underground church existed there, the stronghold of communism was formidable. Much prayer was needed to weaken the enemy's grip so the Word of God could come in. Today, in one of the major cities we visited and prayed over, a printing press has been established. Thousands of Bibles are reaching Chinese believers from that location, and a phenomenal revival is sweeping China, despite continued persecution. When you prayerwalk, you never know what the results of your prayers will be.

Hedge in with Prayer

There are other ways God calls us to pray or proclaim.

Joyce, one of Ruthanne's prayer partners, has not let a single year go by since her children started school when she didn't pray over the school building where they'd be attending classes. "I go to the building, anoint the doors with oil, and pray protection over my children, the teachers, the administrators, and other students," she told us. "Using scripture verses I proclaim God's blessings over that school. Just this year a young girl from another school was kidnapped, raped, and murdered, and it sent a shock wave of fear through our city.

"Less than two weeks later as I was driving home one afternoon I saw in the distance a police helicopter hovering over my daughter's school. I turned down that street and began praying in the Spirit as I drove around the building, which had several police cars around it. Later, I learned the police were looking for a rapist who had escaped from a prison in the next town. They had locked all the schools in the city so students couldn't leave until they felt it was safe. That night I kept waking up throughout the night, crying and praying for the children of our city. These conditions not only call for warfare prayer, but give opportunity to share the good news of God's power and protection with families in the community."

Spirit-filled women who work outside the home also pray for God's purposes to be established in the lives of their co-workers and employers. They are open to share the gospel whenever they are asked. And they let their very lives proclaim God's glory.

Planting Seeds

Sometimes we plant seeds where we work simply by our attitude and demeanor toward co-workers. Other times we have the privilege to reap a harvest. When I (Quin) worked in a newsroom, I felt the Lord targeted two women for me to pray for and eventually to share the Lord with. One was open, the other very closed.

Once I (Ruthanne) was working on a temporary job where I had a very angry, troubled woman as a supervisor. She gave me my work assignments, but otherwise was barely civil toward me. One afternoon during break time I dropped and broke my thermos while pouring a cup of hot tea at my desk. Without a

word I cleaned up the spill, picked up the broken pieces and
threw them away, then went back to my typewriter.

My boss stared at me from her desk nearby. "Didn't I just see
you break your thermos?" she asked. "How can you be so
calm?"

"Getting mad wouldn't do any good," I said, laughing. "No
big deal—I broke it, so I'll do without tea today."

It was nothing heroic, but my reaction seemed to impress
her, and she was much friendlier after that. Before I left that
assignment, she knew I was a Christian, and she respected me. I
gained compassion for her disappointment in her broken marriage, and prayed that someone else would come along and
water the seed I had planted.

Since both of us travel a great deal, sometimes we have
opportunities to share our faith with others on airplanes.
Recently I (Quin) sat next to a woman who said she worked as a
stripper for nightclubs. She had just had breast implant surgery
and was extremely sick as the effects of the anesthesia were still
wearing off. During our plane trip, all I could do was to try to
encourage her and pray silently for her. My heart ached for the
fear and darkness that engulfed her.

In such situations I sometimes paraphrase verses of Scripture
to pray like this: "Lord, open this woman's eyes and turn her
from darkness to light, and from the power of Satan to God, so
that she may receive forgiveness of sins and a place among
those who are sanctified by faith in you" (based on Acts 26:18).

Reaching Out through Hospitality

While you may never travel far, God will put people in your
path whom you can influence for him. One of the best ways
modern-day Christian women can proclaim the Good News is
through hospitality. Using our homes to touch our friends and
neighbors, we may reach people who would never enter a
church.

After the outpouring of the Holy Spirit on the day of Pentecost, believers began meeting in homes to devote themselves to these four things:

- the apostles' teaching
- fellowship
- breaking of bread
- prayer

The homes of those in the Early Church became sanctuaries for teaching, prayer, fellowship, and meals. Hospitality—reaching out to those God puts in your path—is an effective way to win others to the Lord.

The Apostle Peter wrote:

Offer hospitality to one another without grumbling. Each one should use whatever gift he has received to serve others, faithfully administering God's grace in its various forms. (1 Peter 4:9-10)

In the Living Bible it is even more graphic:

Most important of all, continue to show deep love for each other, for love makes up for many of your faults. Cheerfully share your home with those who need a meal or a place to stay for the night. God has given each of you some special abilities; be sure to use them to help each other, passing on to others God's many kinds of blessings. (1 Peter 4:8-10 TLB)

While Peter was encouraging Christians to help other believers, if we are full of God's love, we will find creative ways to use our homes as avenues of sharing the gospel. As in the early church, our homes also can be "little sanctuaries." How many times have you had others come into your home and say, "I feel peace here." Or, "I just like to come into your house—it's so restful." Why is that? Hopefully because the presence of the Lord is there.

The Company of Women

As a member of the company of women commissioned to proclaim the Good News, each one of us has the privilege of allowing the Holy Spirit to help us to do it in a variety of ways— no matter what our age or station in life.

Our society promotes the notion that when you retire, you can finally enjoy doing things to please yourself. This hidden message gives you a false idea that you've done your duty in life—now your can devote your time to travel, camping, shopping, or handcrafts. Yet in the biblical record some of the most important contributions were made by people in their later years.

Many retired people use their gifts and find fulfillment in doing volunteer work in their neighborhoods, mission organizations, nursing homes, orphanages, hospitals, and day care centers. One retired pediatrician went to Guatemala six times a year to establish medical clinics. A shut-in lady knits slippers for a nearby nursing home, another makes caps and blankets for maternity wards, still another takes supper every night to her invalid neighbor. Pastor Lloyd Ogilvie, who at this writing serves as chaplain of the U.S. Senate, says this regarding the secret of a dynamic walk in the Holy Spirit:

Being filled daily by the Spirit is not just for our enjoyment or warm fuzzy feelings, or even our private piety. The Holy Spirit wants to equip us for ministry. Every day. His gifts of love, wisdom, faith, knowledge, discernment, healing, and prophecy to speak forth boldly about our faith—all are given as empowering for our daily cross of service.... There's a tremendous release when we begin to think that a really good day is one in which we've been used to make a difference in the lives of people around us.[5]

Yes, women, we do have a message. We are counted in the host of women who can proclaim the defeat of the enemy and the victory of our Lord Jesus Christ. The Holy Spirit calls and empowers us to take up this challenge and experience Spirit-filled living.

NOTES

ONE
Welcoming the Holy Spirit

1. John Sherrill, *They Speak With Other Tongues*, (Grand Rapids, Mich.: Chosen Books/Fleming H. Revell, 1964, 1985), 90.
2. Sherrill, 90.
3. Sherrill, 130.
4. Gerald Rowlands, "How to Receive the Holy Spirit," *Turning Point II*, (Lynnwood, Wash.: Women's Aglow Fellowship, 1986), 12-13.

TWO
God's Incredible Gift

1. Jack Hayford, "Kingdom Dynamics," *The Spirit-Filled Life Bible*, ed. Jack Hayford (Nashville: Thomas Nelson, 1991), 1622.
2. *Strong's Exhaustive Concordance of the Bible*, (Nashville: Broadman and Holman, 1978), Greek references #1410 & #1411.
3. *The E.W. Bullinger Companion Bible*, (Grand Rapids, Mich.: Zondervan, 1964), reference number 1556.
4. Gerald Rowlands, "How to Receive the Holy Spirit," *Turning Point II*, (Edmonds, Wash.: Women's Aglow Fellowship, 1986), 14.

THREE
Renewal from the Inside Out

1. Gordon D. Fee, *God's Empowering Presence* (Peabody, Mass.: Hendrickson, 1994), 319-320.
2. Catherine Marshall, *The Helper* (Grand Rapids, Mich.: Baker, 1988), 66-67.
3. Charles Finney, *Principles of Salvation* (Minneapolis, Minn.: Bethany House, 1989), sermons originally published 1839-1891, 44, 46.
4. *Strong's,* Greek reference #5483.
5. *Strong's,* Greek reference #630.
6. Corrie ten Boom, *Marching Orders for the End Battle* (Fort Washington, Pa.: Christian Literature Crusade, 1969), 32-33.
7. Dennis and Rita Bennett, *The Holy Spirit and You* (Plainfield, N.J.: Logos, 1971), 77.
8. John White, *Changing on the Inside* (Ann Arbor, Mich.: Servant, 1991), 156.
9. Eileen Wallis, *Queen Take Your Throne* (Columbia, Mo.: Cityhill, 1987), 92.
10. JoAnne Wallace, *Dress With Style* (Old Tappan, N.J.: Fleming Revell, 1983), 13.
11. Eileen Wallis, 63.

FOUR
Why Speak in Tongues?

1. *International Bible Dictionary* (Plainfield, N.J.: Logos, 1977), 335.
2. Stanley M. Horton, *What the Bible Says About the Holy Spirit* (Springfield, Mo.: Gospel Publishing House, 1976) 139, 140.
3. C. Peter Wagner, *Spreading the Fire* (Ventura, Calif.: Regal, 1994), 25.
4. J. Rodman Williams, *The Gift of the Holy Spirit Today* (Plainfield, N.J.: Logos, 1980), 29.

5. Horton, 138-39.
6. Donald Lee Barnett & Jeffrey P. McGregor, *Speaking in Other Tongues: A Scholarly Defense* (Seattle, Wash.: Community Chapel, 1986), Chapter 5, Part V, 228-254.
7. Quoted from Guy Chevreau's book, *Catch the Fire* (Toronto, Canada: Harper Collins, 1995), 78, 79, 82-83.
8. J. Edwin Orr, *The Fervent Prayer* (Chicago, Ill.: Moody, 1974), 200.
9. Stanley Howard Frodsham, *With Signs Following* (Springfield, Mo.: Gospel Publishing House, first edition 1926; quote from revised edition, 1946), 20.
10. Aimee Semple McPherson, *This is That* (Los Angeles, Calif.: Echo Park Evangelistic Association, 1923), 45.
11. McPherson, 50-51.
12. A report of this camp meeting appears in *A Diary of Signs and Wonders* by Maria Woodworth-Etter, (Tulsa, Okla.: Harrison House, 1981), 258-272.
13. H. B. Garlock, *Before We Kill and Eat You,* edited by Ruthanne Garlock, (Dallas, Tex.: CHRIST FOR THE NATIONS, 1974), 100.
14. C. K. Mackintosh, *Genesis to Deuteronomy: Notes on the Pentateuch* (Neptune, N.J.: Loizeaux Brothers, 1972), 58.
15. Horton, 141-142.
16. John White, *When the Spirit Comes with Power* (Ann Arbor, Mich., Servant, 1988), 53.

FIVE
Cultivating the Fruit of the Spirit

1. Herbert Lockyer, *All About the Holy Spirit* (Peabody, Mass.: Hendrickson, 1995), 106, 107. This work was first published as *The Breath of God* by Union Gospel Press, 1949.
2. Fee, 441.
3. Commentary on Romans 5:5, *Spirit-Filled Life Bible,* 1694.

4. Richard J. Foster, *The Challenge of the Disciplined Life* (San Francisco, Calif.: Harper & Row, 1985), 204.

5. W. E. Vine, *Vine's Expository Dictionary of Old and New Testament Words* (Old Tappan, N.J.: Fleming H. Revell, 1981), 169-170.

6. Fee, 449-50.

7. Wallis, 61-62.

8. Notes on Galatians 5:22, *Spirit-Filled Life Bible,* 1780.

9. Fee, 450-51.

10. Fee, 451.

11. William Barclay, *The Letters to the Galatians and Ephesians* (Philadelphia: The Westminster Press, 1976), 51,52.

12. *Strong's Exhaustive Concordance of the Bible,* Greek reference #2904, and *The Reader's Digest Illustrated Dictionary and Concordance of the Bible,* (Reader's Digest Association, 1992), 1219.

13. C. Peter Wagner, *Your Spiritual Gifts Can Help Your Church Grow* (Ventura, Calif.: Regal, 1979, 1994), 83-84.

14. Jane Hansen, "Let's Talk," *Connection* Newsletter, Winter 1995, (Women's Aglow Fellowship, Lynnwood, Wash.), 2.

SIX
The Gifted Woman on a Mission

1. Jack Hayford, *Spirit-Filled: The Overflowing Power of the Holy Spirit* (Wheaton Ill.: Tyndale, 1984), 91.

2. Paul Walker, "Holy Spirit Gifts and Power," *The Spirit-Filled Life Bible,* 2022-4.

3. Walker, 2022-4.

4. Walker, 2022-4. These definitions are condensed from Dr. Walker's more extensive definitions of motivational gifts.

5. Wagner, *Your Spiritual Gifts Can Help Your Church Grow,* 116.

6. The above book by Dr. Wagner can be used for testing. Also, we recommend *Discover Your God-Given Gifts* by Don and Katie Fortune, (Grand Rapids, Mich.: Fleming H. Revell/Baker, 1987).

7. Annie Chapman, *Smart Women Keep It Simple* (Minneapolis, Minn.: Bethany, 1992), 188.

8. Fee, 160.

9. Wagner, *Your Spiritual Gifts Can Help Your Church Grow*, 31-32.

10. Definitions of the nine gifts of the Spirit taken from *The Spirit-Filled Life Bible*, 1736-37; notes by Donald Pickerill, Life Bible College, San Demas, Calif.

11. Gordon Lindsay, *Gifts of the Spirit* (Dallas, Tex.: CHRIST FOR THE NATIONS, 1989), Volume 1, 74-75, 80.

12. H. B. Garlock, 109-110.

13. Smith Wigglesworth, *The Anointing of His Spirit*, ed. Wayne Warner (Ann Arbor, Mich.: Servant, 1994), 91.

14. Cindy Jacobs, *The Voice of God* (Ventura, Calif.: Regal, 1992), 191, 193.

15. Lindsay, Volume 3, 135.

16. Vine, 314-315.

17. Dr. Fuchsia Pickett, *Presenting the Holy Spirit* (Shippensburg, Pa.: Destiny Image, 1994), Volume 2, 75.

18. Lindsay, Volume 4, 77.

19. Fee, 706.

SEVEN

The Unshakable Spirit-Filled Warrior

1. *The E. W. Bullinger Companion Bible*, notes on Ephesians 4:14 and 6:11, 1766.

2. Arthur Mathews, *Born For Battle* (Robesonia, Pa.: OMF Books, 1978), 51-53.

3. These ideas taken from lecture notes and Dean Sherman's book, *Spiritual Warfare for Every Christian* (Seattle, Wash.: Frontline Communications, 1990).

4. For suggestions for using the Word of God in spiritual warfare, see our book *The Spiritual Warrior's Prayer Guide* (Ann Arbor, Mich.: Servant, 1992).

5. *Strong's,* Hebrew reference #8104.
6. Vine, Volume 4, 201.
7. Joan Morton, *Women of Prayer* (Lynnwood, Wash.: Womens Aglow Fellowship, 1993), 76.
8. Morton, 79.
9. See our book *How To Pray for Family and Friends* (Ann Arbor, Mich.: Servant, 1990).
10. *Spirit-Filled Life Bible,* 1535.

EIGHT

Praying in the Spirit

1. E.W. Bullinger, *Word Studies on the Holy Spirit* (Grand Rapids, Mich.: Kregel, 1979), 162. [Originally published as *The Giver and His Gifts* in London, England by Eyre & Spottiswoode, 1905.]
2. Arthur Wallis, *Pray in the Spirit* (Fort Washington, Pa.: Christian Literature Crusade, 1970), 86.
3. Johannes Facius, *Explaining Intercession* (Tonbridge, Kent, England: Sovereign World Ltd., 1993), 39-40.
4. Fee, 580, 586.
5. ten Boom, 33-34.
6. Ted Haggard, "A Pastor's Prayer Principles," *Ministries Today,* (Lake Mary, Fla.: Strang Communications Co., November-December, 1994), 17.

NINE

Our Expectations—God's Intervention

1. Freda Lindsay, *My Diary Secrets* (Dallas, Tex.: CHRIST FOR THE NATIONS, 1976, 1982), 52-53, from 4th edition, 1982.
2. Dr. Charles H. Kraft, *Christianity With Power* (Ann Arbor, Mich.: Servant, 1989), 124.
3. Kraft, 149.

4. Kraft, 166.
5. Dr. Larry Crabb, *Inside Out* (Colorado Springs, Colo.: Navpress, 1988), 88.

TEN
Walking in the Spirit

1. W. E. Vine, Volume 3, 195.
2. David Wilkerson, "What It Means to Walk in the Spirit," *Times Square Church Pulpit Series,* August 15, 1994, 1.
3. A. B. Simpson, "Walking in the Spirit," *Herald of His Coming,* February 1995, 5. [Reprinted from the book by A. B. Simpson, *The Gentle Love of the Holy Spirit* (Camp Hill Pa.: Christian Publications, 1983).]
4. Richard Exley, *The Rhythm of Life* (Tulsa, Okla.: Harrison House, 1987), 107-08.
5. Elizabeth Alves, *The Mighty Warrior: A Guide to Effective Prayer* (Bulverde, Tex.: Intercessors International, 1992), 69-70.
6. Alves, 74-77.
7. Wilkerson, 4.

ELEVEN
Avoiding the Pitfalls

1. *Spirit-Filled Life Bible,* 1666.
2. Phil Phillips, *Angels, Angels, Angels* (Lancaster, Pa.: Starburst, 1995), 136, 137.
3. Wagner, *Your Spiritual Gifts Can Help Your Church Grow,* 93-94.
4. Dick Mills, *A Good Word For You* (Orange, Calif.: Dick Mills Ministries, 1996), 1.
5. Lance Lambert, *Experiencing Spiritual Protection* (West Sussex, England: Sovereign World Limited 1991), 47.

TWELVE
Proclaiming the Good News!

1. Steve Hawthorne and Graham Kendrick, *Prayerwalking* (Orlando, Fla., Creation House, 1993), 15-17.
2. Mary Lance Sisk, "Love Your Neighbor As Yourself— Restoration of Your Neighborhood," (cassette tape distributed by Aglow International, Edmonds, Wash., 1995).
3. Hawthorne and Kendrick, 129.
4. Hawthorne and Kendrick, 126-130.
5. Lloyd Ogilvie, *The Greatest Counselor in the World* (Ann Arbor, Mich.: Servant, 1994), 186.

Recommended
Reading
List

⚜

Aglow International. *Women of Prayer: Released to the Nations.* (an anthology on prayer) Lynnwood, Wash.: Women's Aglow Fellowship, 1993.

Alves, Elizabeth. *The Mighty Warrior: A Guide to Effective Prayer.* Bulverde, Tex.: Intercessors International, 1987, 1995.

Bennett, Dennis and Rita. *The Holy Spirit and You.* Plainfield, N.J.: Logos, 1971.

Christenson, Evelyn. *Lord, Change Me.* Wheaton, Ill.: Victor, 1981.

Elliot, Elizabeth. *Keep a Quiet Heart.* Ann Arbor, Mich.: Servant, 1993.

Exley, Richard. *The Rhythm of Life.* Tulsa, Okla.: Harrison House, 1987.

Fee, Gordon D. *God's Empowering Presence.* Peabody, Mass.: Hendrickson, 1994.

Fortune, Don and Katie. *Discover Your God-Given Gifts.* Grand Rapids: Fleming H. Revell/Baker, 1987.

Frodsham, Stanley Howard. *With Signs Following.* Springfield, Mo.: Gospel Publishing, 1946.

Garlock, H.B. *Before We Kill and Eat You.* Dallas: CHRIST FOR THE NATIONS, 1974.

Hansen, Jane. *Inside A Woman.* Lynnwood, Wash.: Aglow, 1992.

Hawthorne, Steve and Graham Kendrick. *Prayerwalking.* Orlando, Fla.: Creation House, 1993.

Hayford, Jack, ed. *Spirit-Filled: The Overflowing Power of the Holy Spirit.* Wheaton, Ill.: Tyndale, 1984.

Horton, Stanley M. *What the Bible Says About the Holy Spirit.* Springfield, Mo.: Gospel Publishing House, 1976.

Jacobs, Cindy. *Possessing the Gates of the Enemy.* Tarrytown, N.Y.: Chosen Books/Fleming H. Revell, 1991.

Jacobs, Cindy. *The Voice of God.* Ventura, Calif.: Regal, 1995.

Lindsay, Freda. *My Diary Secrets.* Dallas: CHRIST FOR THE NATIONS, 1976, 1982.

Lindsay, Gordon. *Gifts of the Spirit.* Volumes 1-4, Dallas, Tex.: CHRIST FOR THE NATIONS, 1989.

Lord, Peter. *Hearing God.* Grand Rapids, Mich.: Baker, 1988.

Lush, Jean. *Emotional Phases of a Woman's Life.* Grand Rapids, Mich.: Fleming H. Revell/Baker, 1987, 1993.

Marshall, Catherine. *The Helper.* Grand Rapids, Mich.: Chosen Books, 1978.

Mathews, Arthur. *Born For Battle.* Robesonia, Pa.: OMF, 1978.

McPherson, Aimee Semple. *This is That.* Los Angeles: Echo Park Evangelistic Association, 1923.

Ogilvie, Lloyd. *The Greatest Counselor in the World.* Ann Arbor, Mich.: Servant, 1994.

Phillips, Phil. *Angels, Angels, Angels.* Lancaster, Pa.: Starburst, 1995.

Pickett, Fuchsia. *Presenting the Holy Spirit.* volumes 1 and 2, Shippensburg, Pa.: Destiny Image, 1994.

Sherrer, Quin and Ruthanne Garlock. *How to Pray for Your Family and Friends.* Ann Arbor, Mich.: Servant, 1990.

Sherman, Dean. *Spiritual Warfare for Every Christian.* Seattle: Frontline Communications, 1990.

Sherrill, John. *They Speak With Other Tongues.* Grand Rapids, Mich.: Chosen Books/Fleming H. Revell, 1964, 1985.

ten Boom, Corrie. *Marching Orders for the End Battle.* Fort Washington, Pa.: Christian Literature Crusade, 1969.

Wagner, C. Peter. *The Acts of the Holy Spirit series.* Ventura, Calif.: Regal, 1994, 1995.

Wagner, C. Peter. *Your Spiritual Gifts Can Help Your Church Grow.* Ventura, Calif.: Regal, 1979, 1994.

Wallis, Eileen. *Queen Take Your Throne.* Columbia, Mo.: Cityhill, 1987.

Wallis, Arthur. *Pray in the Spirit.* Fort Washington, Pa.: Christian Literature Crusade, 1970.

White, John. *Changing on the Inside.* Ann Arbor, Mich.: Servant, 1991.

White, John. *When the Spirit Comes with Power.* Ann Arbor, Mich.: Servant, 1988.

Wigglesworth, Smith *The Anointing of His Spirit.* Wayne Warner, ed. Ann Arbor, Mich.: Servant, 1994.

Woodworth-Etter, Maria. *A Diary of Signs and Wonders.* (re printed by Harrison House, Tulsa, Okla.) 1981.